BLESSED BROKEN & SCARED

Becoming Eucharist
for a Starving World

J. BRIAN PUSATERI

BLESSED, BROKEN, AND SCARED
Becoming Eucharist for a Starving World
Copyright © 2021 J. Brian Pusateri

Published by J. Brian Pusateri

All rights reserved. With the exception of short excerpts from critical reviews, no part of this book may be reproduced or transmitted in any form or by any means whatsoever without permission in writing from the publisher. For information, contact J Brian Pusateri at brian@brokendoorministries.com

Scripture texts in this work are taken from the *New American Bible, revised edition* © 2010, 1991, 1986, 1970 Confraternity of Christian Doctrine, Washington, D.C., and are used by permission of the copyright owner. All Rights Reserved. No part of the *New American Bible* may be reproduced in any form without permission in writing from the copyright owner.

Every reasonable effort has been made to determine copyright holders of exerted and quoted materials and to secure permissions as needed. In many cases, the principle of "Fair Use" is applicable. If any copyrighted materials have been inadvertently used without proper credit being given, please notify the publisher, J Brian Pusateri, at brian@brokendoorministries.com so that future printings may be corrected accordingly.

ISBN: 9798789563625

Cover and interior design by Exodus Design.
www.ExodusDesign.com

*This book is dedicated to my wife,
Mary Beth Pusateri.*

We have been together for nearly 50 years. She is my best friend, a source of inspiration, an example of Christ-like love, the wind beneath my wings, and the mother of our wonderful children.

Without her love, this book would not have been possible.

TABLE OF CONTENTS

Acknowledgments	I
Introduction	III
The Broken Door	**1**
Self-Knowledge	3
Adam and Eve Syndrome	7
The Lizard	11
Exercise One - The Purple Paper Exercise	15
Recalculating the Route	19
Parable of the Broken Door	25
Blessed	**31**
God's Unwarranted Love	33
Soldier/Priest Story	37
Music Meditation	39
Broken	**41**
Broken by Sin	43
Wounded by the World	51
Music Meditation	55
Scared	**57**
Masks	59
Exercise Two - The Yellow Paper Exercise	65
The Encounter with God That Changed My Life!	71

Summary of Being Scared	77
Music Meditation	55
Shared	**81**
Our Call To Be Eucharist	83
Living in Community	89
Three Personality Traits	95
Wounded Healers	101
Exercise Three - The Mirror Exercise	103
Moonglow	107
A Broken Door	109
Encountering Christ in Our Vulnerability	111
Two Heroes	115
The First Hero	117
The Second Hero	121
Inward-Upward-Outward	125
Called	**129**
The Call	131
A Sea of Purple	135
Becoming Eucharist	141
The Blood of Christ	147
Music Meditation	151
Haunted by the Story of the Little Boy	153
Going Forth	163

Standing in the Storms of Life   167
Endnotes   **171**

ACKNOWLEDGMENTS

I have so many people to thank for their help and support during the time I wrote this book. I begin by thanking my wife and children, who support and affirm me in my ministry work. I want to thank the men who have been members of my Cursillo Friendship Groups in Ocala, Fl., Greenville, SC, Hendersonville, NC, and Mountain Hill Community Church. I want to thank my dear friend Joseph Galloway, who is the author of *The Broken Door*. Joe encouraged me to write this book.

I want to thank Bob Lange and Bob Dylewski for helping me formulate the Blessed, Broken, and Scared retreat format. I want to thank the Board of Directors of Broken Door Ministries, who have graciously given their time to make this ministry possible. I want to thank Annie Coletta for her initial help with editing and formatting. I want to thank my friends who reviewed my first manuscript and offered their constructive suggestions. I want to thank Pastor Lee Noris of Mountain Hill Community Church for the countless hours we have spent discussing the ecumenical aspects of this message and our faith. I want to especially thank Fr. Nick Mormando for suggesting that I go on the retreat that changed my life and Fr. Martin Schratz, who has been my pastor, spiritual advisor, confessor, and my friend. Finally, I want to give thanks and praise to my Lord and Savior Jesus Christ for showering His abundant love and mercy on me every day.

INTRODUCTION

It was the week before Thanksgiving in November of 2011. A dimly lit spotlight illuminated the Tabernacle as I knelt before it to pray at 3 am. This was the third day of an eight-day silent Christian retreat. Little did I know that what was about to transpire over the next fifteen minutes would not only change my life but also touch and change the lives of thousands of others around the world.

In the stillness of the night, on the second-floor chapel of the Magnificat House nestled on the shores of Tampa Bay, with only the hushed sound of waves lapping the shoreline. God spoke plainly to my heart. *"Brian, if you want to heal, you have to tell someone you are broken."* These words changed my life forever! In this book, I will attempt to explain why.

Allow me to ask you some very personal questions. Do you have any area of brokenness in your life that is known only to you? Do you harbor some well-guarded secrets? What impact would it have on you if you shared your brokenness with others? How might it impact them? How could sharing your brokenness change the world for Christ? It can! I will endeavor to explain how God's message to me can change your life, too. I am convinced that the message God placed on my heart that day is also the message that He wants to place in yours as well. I hope that it will change your life too.

Blessed, Broken, and Scared might seem like an odd title. I hope as you read through this book, you will discover that this title is not as odd as it first appears. My aim is to use words to draw a picture for you, much like the famous mural of "The Last Supper" by Leonardo da Vinci located inside Milan's Santa Maria delle Grazie monastery. During the meal, as related in the gospel stories, Jesus performed four simple yet very profound actions. And what is contained in those actions and our own reaction to them is what this book is about. We will explore the implications of how the Last Supper challenges us to live our lives in such a way that we actually become the sacred food of Jesus Christ for the lost and broken people of the world—for those people who are starving to receive Him.

Writing this book took me almost five years. Learning what to write took me a lifetime. And this story you are about to read recaps my journey of faith. My sincere hope is that you will discover a few things that can help you see and understand God's calling in your life more clearly. I will strive to make the point that true Christian community is an essential part of God's plan for each of us. But the most important point I hope to make is this: as long as we remain broken and scared people, we will fall short of becoming the Eucharistic people God intended us to be.

If we are to become a eucharistic people, then we need to understand the meaning of Eucharist. The word Eucharist comes to us from the Greek word *eucharistia*, which means *thanksgiving*. Throughout this book, we will explore what it means to *"be"* a people of thanksgiving.

To be clear, I am writing this book for all Christians. While the word Eucharist is primarily used by Catholics, don't let that concern you at this point. The eucharistic meal—this meal of thanksgiving—is also commonly referred to as "The Lord's Supper" or simply "Communion." I will be using all these terms interchangeably throughout this book.

I realize that all Christians do not share a common view concerning this meal of thanksgiving. While many deeply faithful Christians believe in the real presence of Christ's body and blood in the form of consecrated bread and wine, other Christians who are as deeply faithful see this meal as a symbolic or spiritual presence of our Lord.

With respect to each viewpoint, however, the underlying premise remains constant. In much the same way as Catholics believe that the bread and wine are transformed into our Lord's body and blood, all Christians, regardless of our religious affiliations, are called to their own transformation. And through this conversion, we are then challenged to be Christ to others.

The Jews ate the gift of heavenly manna to survive their journey in the desert. Ponder how much more life-giving it can be in our own wilderness journeys than to be nourished by the gift of our Lord through His people. We are called to be Christ to others so that as a eucharistic meal for them, they can be nourished by Him and come to believe in God's Son, Jesus. And they, too, can have everlasting life. How privileged and grateful we are to share this meal of thanksgiving.

In Matthew 26:26, it states, *"While they were eating, Jesus took bread, said the blessing, broke it, and giving it to his disciples said, 'Take and eat; this is my body.'"* Through this action, Jesus instituted the first eucharistic meal. The bread was taken, blessed, broken, and shared. This book and its message are built upon the importance of these four words.

I sincerely hope that as you make your way through the words I have written, you will learn that you, too, are taken by God, blessed by God, broken, and created by God to be shared. When we fall short of this, we cease to be the eucharistic people our God calls us to be.

Understanding and coming to grips with our own brokenness is a very important part of our Christian journey. If, however, we never progress beyond this self-awareness, our introspection is nothing short of a useless navel-gazing exercise. If we never progress beyond our own introspection, we will not become a eucharistic people. Instead, we will remain BLESSED, BROKEN, and SCARED. Blessed, broken, and scared is not Eucharist.

I chose to name this book *Blessed, Broken, and Scared* because, sadly, this is where many of us are stuck. If we are to become communion for others, then we must go through a conversion to become a Blessed, Broken, and SHARED people.

Together let's embark on a journey to see how we can become the Eucharistic people God calls us to be.

THE BROKEN DOOR

SELF-KNOWLEDGE

In his book confessions, ST. Augustine wrote, "Lord, let me know myself; let me know you."[1] This double-knowledge, as it is sometimes referred to, can be an important part of the Christian conversion experience. Because Christian conversion is a life-long progressive journey, we should ask ourselves these two questions on a regular basis in order to assess our progress:

> What did God reveal to me about me this week that I never knew before?

> What did God reveal to me about Him this week that I never knew before?

Seeking the answers to these questions will help us to see if we are making progress as Christians. It is important, however, that we keep in mind that we can't stop with just knowledge. No, we are called to much more than knowledge of self and knowledge of God. As Christians, we are called to be people of action. This book is intended to help you with your own personal introspection so that you can use that knowledge to bring about change in your own life and the lives of others.

A few years back, my parish, Immaculate Conception Parish in Hendersonville, North Carolina, adopted a new parish mission. Notice that I wrote *mission,* not *mission statement*. The parish leaders felt that parish mission statements often merely resided on paper. The leaders wanted a mission that would live in the heart of every member of the parish. After nine months of work and with the Holy Spirit's guidance, they gave birth to this mission: *We are a Joyful Catholic community, of disciples of Jesus Christ, moved by love to seek the lost and broken and bring them home.* In keeping with the ecumenical spirit in which this book is written, I would like to propose broadening of this mission to: *We are a Joyful Christian community, of disciples of Jesus Christ, moved by love to seek the lost and broken and bring them home.* I hope you can agree with me that this could and should be the mission of all Christian churches and therefore, our personal mission as well.

This mission is a good starting point. The mission begs the question, just who are those lost and broken people? Is it possible that we (yes, you and I) are those lost and broken people? At first, the people on the committee at my parish, tasked with the job of creating this mission, were inclined to think that the lost and broken people were on the outside of the church doors. It soon became evident that the phrase "lost and broken" included everyone—both those inside and those outside of the doors. Hopefully, as you make your way through this book, you will begin to see yourself included in the phrase "lost and broken people." That is, if it is not already clearly apparent to you.

We are challenged to understand that we are both called to seek the lost and broken and, at the same time, acknowledge that we, too, are lost and broken. We are called both into the action of seeking others while we simultaneously accept the reality that we ourselves are in need of being sought and found.

On August 16, 1905, The London Daily News invited prominent philosophers to write an essay to address this one question, "What'swrong with the world today?" G. K. Chesterton responded with an utterly profound answer. Here is the essence of what he had to say:

In one sense, and that the eternal sense, the thing is plain. The answer to the question, "What is Wrong?" is, or should be, "I am wrong." Until a man can give that answer his idealism is only a hobby."[2]

G. K. Chesterton

Chesterton had the insight to see that the world's problems were not caused by everyone else. He knew that every person had some culpability in the collective problems of the world.

It is vitally important that we each examine and acknowledge our role in the collective brokenness of the world. I will explain then share my view as to how our brokenness might also be an important part of the solution. Moving from a broken people to a eucharistic people is the conversion process we are called to undertake.

Are you ready to begin?

ADAM AND EVE SYNDROME

Let me set the stage for what will become a theme throughout this book with a simple little story. It is the story of Little Johnny and the Cookies.

Johnny's mother had just finished baking some fresh chocolate chip cookies. The aroma of those cookies was wafting through the house when little Johnny came bounding into the kitchen. Johnny's mother had just put the last cookie in the cookie jar. She had other work to do in a different room in the house, so she instructed Johnny, "Johnny, do not get into these cookies."

With that, she left the kitchen, leaving Johnny precariously alone with the tempting cookies.

What do you think Johnny did? Do you think that Johnny got into those cookies? Of course, he did! Very soon thereafter, Johnny's mom walked back into the kitchen, and she noticed that the lid was off the cookie jar. She addressed Johnny with these words, "Johnny, did you get into these cookies?"

Johnny responded, "No, mommy, I didn't get into the cookies."

Asking more sternly the second time, Johnny's mom said, "Johnny, now don't lie to me. Did you get into these cookies?"

Looking up at his mom Johnny said, "My sister Sally said that

I could have one."

Even more sternly, Johnny's mom asked her question for the final time, "Johnny, did— —you— — eat— — one —- of —- the —- cookies?"

Looking up at his mom with sad puppy dog eyes, Johnny said, "Yes, mommy, but I will never do it again!"

Does anyone believe that this will be the last time that little Johnny will sneak a cookie from the cookie jar? Human nature tells me that Johnny will sneak many more cookies in his future.

Why did I tell you this story? I did so because the story depicts what I refer to as the Adam and Eve syndrome. What do I mean by that? Let's take a look in the Garden of Eden from Genesis 3:1-13

Now the snake was the most cunning of all the wild animals that the LORD God had made. He asked the woman, "Did God really say, 'You shall not eat from any of the trees in the garden'?" The woman answered the snake, "We may eat of the fruit of the trees in the garden; it is only about the fruit of the tree in the middle of the garden that God said, 'You shall not eat it or even touch it, or else you will die.'" But the snake said to the woman, "You certainly will not die! God knows well that when you eat of it your eyes will be opened and you will be like gods, who know good and evil." The woman saw that the tree was good for food and pleasing to the eyes and the tree was desirable for gaining wisdom. So she took some of its fruit and ate it; and she also gave some to her husband, who was with her, and he ate it. Then the eyes of both of them were opened, and they knew that they were naked; so they sewed fig leaves together and made loincloths for themselves.

When they heard the sound of the LORD God walking about in the garden at the breezy time of the day, the man and his wife hid themselves from the LORD God among the trees of the garden. The LORD God then called to the man and asked him: Where are you? He answered, "I heard you in the garden; but I was afraid, because I was naked, so I hid." Then God asked: Who told you that you were naked? Have you eaten from the tree of which I had forbidden you to eat? The man replied, "The woman whom you put here with me—she gave me fruit from the tree, so I ate it." The LORD God then asked the woman: What is this you have done? The woman answered, "The snake tricked me, so I ate it."

Can you see the similarities between the story of Little Johnny and the Cookies and the story of Adam and Eve in the Garden of Eden? Both Little Johnny and Adam and Eve disobeyed what they were told to do. When confronted with their wrongdoing, Johnny tried to hide the truth, and Adam and Eve attempted to hide themselves. When pressed for an explanation, Johnny and Adam and Eve tried to blame someone else. Eventually, they all owned up to the truth, but we know that this was not the last time that Johnny nor Adam and Eve disobeyed.

The Adam and Eve syndrome looks like this:

Do something wrong

Get caught

Blame someone else

Admit to the truth

Promise to never do it again

DO IT AGAIN!

Does this syndrome sound familiar in your own life? Are there things that you have done wrong and then promised God that you would never do again, only to do that very same thing over and over? I feel it's safe to assume that ever since Adam and Eve, all human beings have fallen into this trap.

Now let me ask you for a moment of honesty. If you are a Catholic, is it your experience that every time you go to receive the Sacrament of Reconciliation, you find yourself confessing the same sin? If you are not a Catholic, do you find yourself sitting in the quiet of your home looking up towards the heavens and saying, "Yes, God, I did it again?"

I once said to my confessor, "I might as well record my confession on a CD and just mail it to you once a month because it seems like I always have the same sins to confess."

I believe each of us is all too keenly aware of what we struggle with in life. Would you like to discover a method for breaking the habit, or at least reducing the frequency of your recurring sin? I hope I can successfully demonstrate that you can find freedom and healing from the sins that have you in chains. I have!

As you will see in later chapters, admitting our brokenness is the first step.

THE LIZARD

In 2 Corinthians 12:9, it is written, *"But he said to me, 'My grace is sufficient for you, for power is made perfect in weakness.' I will rather boast most gladly of my weaknesses, in order that the power of Christ may dwell with me."*

It is true that we are weak people. Like St. Paul says in Romans 7:15-20, we do the things we don't want to do. As we just read in the previous chapter, we promised not to do it, but we do it again. Often, it seems we become very comfortable in our recurring sin.

The Bible tells us, *"All have sinned and are deprived of the glory of God."* (Romans 3:23) The passage above tells us that God's power is made perfect through our weakness. In his book, *The Great Divorce*, C.S. Lewis uses some interesting characters to metaphorically depict how God can work through our weakness.

In his somewhat strange account, there is a bus traveling through hell on its way to Heaven. The characters on the bus are ghost-like figures. They are transparent. The symbolism of a lizard on a ghost's shoulder is used to depict the recurring sin in our lives.

One of the ghosts, standing just outside the gate of Heaven, has a red lizard with a twitching tail sitting on his shoulder. The lizard is whispering in the ghost's ear when an angel approaches. The ghost tries to quiet the lizard to no avail. Despite being told to shut up, the lizard continues to incessantly whisper in the ghost's ear. The ghost understands that he cannot enter Heaven with the lizard whispering temptations to him.

An angel approaches the ghost and asks him if he can make the lizard be quiet. The ghost says yes. The angel steps forward and says, *"Then I will kill him."* The ghost responds by saying, *"You didn't say anything about killing him at first. I hardly meant to bother you with anything so drastic as that."*[3]

You see, over the years, the ghost and the lizard had become like friends. They had been together for a long while. Keep in mind here, the lizard represents the recurring sin in the man's life. Despite their long friendship, the ghost really wants to enter heaven. The angel cannot kill the lizard without the express permission of the ghost. Eventually, he reluctantly allows the angel to kill the lizard.

Lewis depicts something very important at this point in his story. He masterfully describes the killing of the lizard as a painful process. The ghost fears that he too might die when the angel's burning hands kill the lizard. Isn't this how we sometimes feel when we try to break away from our recurring sinfulness? We become so attached to our pet sins, that trying to break free from them can be quite a painful process.

Since permission is granted, the angel steps forward to kill the lizard. The ghost willingly endures the pain. Suddenly the ghost-like figure is transformed into a strong young man, and the lizard is transformed into a magnificent silvery-white stallion with a mane and tail of gold. The young man leaps onto the stallion, and together they ride off into the heavenly land.

C.S. Lewis has masterfully painted a scene for us whereby the ghost's recurring sin, the lizard, is transformed into a white stallion that the man rides to the mountain of God. Could it be possible that by admitting and confronting our brokenness, we may, in fact, discover the Stallion that God has prepared for us to ride into Heaven? Going forward, I will explain how that can happen.

EXERCISE ONE

THE PURPLE PAPER EXERCISE

During the retreats, I stop and invite the participants to take part in a little exercise. I want to invite you to participate as well. **Please do not skip this important step. The book will lose its meaning if you do.** This is a critically important exercise and one that I will be referring back to throughout the remainder of the book.

Please search for a small 3-by-5-inch piece of purple paper. If you can't find a purple paper, how about an index card and write the word *Purple* on the top of your paper so that you will know what I am referring to as we journey through the remainder of the book. There is also a card on the last page of the book that you can cut out and use for this exercise.

I'm going to ask you to write some things down on both sides of the paper. It is important that you only write on side one until I instruct you to flip your paper over and write on side two.

Purple Paper	(Back)

For privacy purposes, this is your chance to develop your own form of encrypted hieroglyphics. Due to the sensitive answers that you will be recording, I encourage you to write your answers so that they mean something to you but not to anyone else who might stumble upon and read your paper.

If your answer is yes, to any of the following questions, please make a note of it on *side one* of your paper.

Is there anyone in your life that you are struggling to forgive?

Are you struggling with grief caused by the death of a family member or friend?

Is loneliness something that you struggle with?

Are health issues, either your own or those of someone close to you, weighing you down and causing you to have anxiety or fear?

Are you experiencing marital strife?

Are you experiencing family strife?

Are you experiencing financial difficulties?

Have you had to endure abuse in your life? (physical, sexual, verbal bullying)

Are there any other issues weighing you down that are outside of your control and not caused by you?

Now please flip your paper over to **side two**. This will most likely be a difficult and maybe painful answer to write down.

What is/are the habitual recurring sin/sins in your life that most weigh you down and you constantly find yourself struggling to break free of?

I want to make an important distinction. I am *not* asking you to write down your *worst sin* ever nor some sin(s) from your past that you can't forget. I specifically want you to record the sin(s) that if you confess it/them today, you will soon be back to confess the same one(s) again next time. What is /are the sin(s) that recur in your life and cloud your relationship with God?

Now, please place your paper in a safe place. Can I suggest that you might want to use your Purple Paper as your bookmark? In any case, you will want to keep it until you have finished reading this book.

RECALCULATING THE ROUTE

Have you either driven your car and relied upon GPS to get you to your destination or ridden in a car with someone else who was relying upon GPS? If so, let me pose this question: If you are driving along and your GPS tells you to make a right-hand turn, but you fail to make the turn and continue going straight, what does your GPS tell you to do? Mine tells me to make a U-turn if possible. If you fail to make a U-turn and you ignore the fact that the GPS told you to turn right, what will the GPS say next? Mine says, "Recalculating the route."

With this brief review of the GPS navigational instructions in mind, I want to share with you a personal story. Before I tell the story, allow me to give you a little background information.

I grew up in the small town of Norwalk, Ohio. I am someone who is commonly referred to as a "cradle Catholic." I was baptized in a Catholic Church, and I have been a Catholic throughout my entire life. I attended 12 years of Catholic schooling at St. Paul's Catholic school in Norwalk.

I always felt close to our Lord, and my Catholic faith was important to me even from a very early age. As early as an eighth-grader, I began to feel a tug on my heart to investigate the possibility of attending Holy Spirit Seminary, the high school

Catholic seminary in Toledo, Ohio. I, along with a few of my friends, packed ourselves into a station wagon, and one of the mothers drove us on our 60-mile trip to investigate this seminary. Even at this young age, while I was visiting the seminary, I felt God calling me into the priesthood and that I should attend that high school. Although I felt this calling, I chose to ignore it, and I finished my four years of high school back at St. Paul's in my hometown.

Fast-forward now to my senior year in high school, I was still feeling this tug or calling from God to pursue the priesthood. I spent time during the summer of 1975, immediately following my senior year, visiting with other priests, and discerning this call.

Before telling you the outcome of my discernment, I need to back up a little and fill in an important detail. In my sophomore year, I began to date a girl who, at that time, was a freshman. We continued to date each other throughout my high school years.

Now, let's go back to my discernment. I was fairly certain that God was calling me into the ordained life of the priesthood. That meant that I needed to break off the relationship with my girlfriend. So, I did. But that didn't last long.

Soon after breaking up and telling friends and family that I wanted to enter the seminary, I reversed my course of action. I made the decision that I could not possibly envision life without my girlfriend. I made my decision—and I ignored God's call. I decided against the seminary, and soon thereafter, I was dating this same girl again. We were married just two years later. That was 44 years ago, and we remain happily married to this day.

Okay, with all of that as the backdrop, let's delve further into my story. I mentioned that in November of 2011, I was fortunate to have the opportunity to go on an eight-day silent retreat at a place called the House of Prayer. It was run by the Marian Servants of Divine Providence in Clearwater, Florida. This was to be a silent Ignatian Retreat.

An Ignatian Retreat is an intense, structured experience based upon the teachings of St. Ignatius. For over 400 years, multitudes have been blessed through the meditations, prayers, and various exercises authored by St. Ignatius of Loyola. Each retreatant is guided by a Spiritual Director, who assigns scriptures to pray and meditate upon relating to various themes, such as God's love, mercy, and our calling to serve.

As a retreatant, I spent one hour each day with my Spiritual Director and the remaining 23 hours of the day in silence. This routine would be repeated each day for eight days.

I've told you about what I experienced on the third night, but now let me share a bit more. On the second night of the retreat, I was kneeling all alone in the small chapel next to my second-floor bedroom in the Magnificat House. It was around 3:00 A.M. Directly before me was a Tabernacle containing consecrated hosts, which we as Catholics believe to be the true presence of Jesus Christ in the form of bread. In this eerie silence, while deep in prayer, I suddenly felt God speaking directly to my heart. Although I did not hear His audible voice, His words were quite palpable to my soul. This is what I heard, *"Brian, if you ever wondered if I was truly calling you into the priesthood all those many years ago, I was!"*

He went on to say, *"Just to be clear, you chose sex over Me."*

I knew in an instant what God meant. Back in 1975, during my contemplation of the priesthood at the age of 18, I didn't feel that I would be capable of accepting the priestly vow of celibacy. That is and was my main reason for turning my back on God's call at that time in my life. His word cut the silence like a knife as I knelt in prayer. I was moved to tears.

God, however, did not leave me in despair. He continued to speak to my heart. This is what I heard next, *"Brian, even though you rejected my call, I have blessed you abundantly throughout your life. I have blessed you with a wonderful wife, seven children, two of whom are with me in Heaven, and five which I left in your care, I have blessed you with a successful career, good friends, good health, and a deep faith. But Brian, make no mistake,* **I AM STILL CALLING YOU!"**

At that moment, my life was about to be changed forever. I knew God was right. He had, in fact, called me into the priesthood; He had just reaffirmed this to me. I also knew that He had indeed abundantly blessed my life. At that moment, God became my GPS. What I heard in the stillness of that night on the shores of Tampa Bay at this beautiful House of Prayer was *"recalculating the route."*

I knew that I had failed to heed His call back in 1975; this time in 2011, I was not about to make the same mistake again. I broke the quiet of the night by spontaneously responding to God's call with these words from a song that I had sung many times on my Christian journey. I said, *"Here I am Lord, it is I Lord, I have heard you calling in the night. I will go Lord, if you lead me, I will hold your people in my heart."*

I found this experience to be quite reassuring because God did not give up on me after just one call. God doesn't give up on us when we head the wrong way down the road of life. He simply recalculates our route.

I was 54 years old when I went on this retreat. Therefore, it is safe to say that for 54 years, I did all the talking. During the eight days of this silent retreat, I finally gave God the opportunity to talk while I listened. He had much to say. I will write more about my experience at The House of Prayer in later chapters, but for now, let me reiterate that this was a life-changing experience.

Let me ask you, have there ever been times in life when you have rejected Godn't call?

PARABLE OF THE BROKEN DOOR

Unbeknownst to me, God had already begun to put into motion the changes that were going to occur while on that silent retreat. A couple of months before the retreat, I responded to the Holy Spirit's prompting to write a short inspirational email to 15 men that I knew from church. I had no idea that this would soon become a weekly event – now over 500 messages, praise God. I call these messages 4th *Day Letters.* By the grace of God, they are read around the globe by Christians of many denominations.

One of those weekly messages was like no other. It was the only message that I was inspired to write in the form of a parable.

In the crisp cool of a pre-dawn spring morning, bright stars illuminating the clear sky, I was getting into my hot tub on our back deck. I literally had one leg in the hot tub and one leg outside. All of a sudden, the entire message of what would become known as the *Parable of the Broken Door* flooded into my thoughts. I remember saying, "Lord, don't let me forget this before I dry off and make my way to my computer." What follows next is the message that I was inspired to write.

The Parable of the Broken Door
For several years you had been searching for the perfect home in the mountains. On this day, you sat in the passenger seat as the

real estate agent drove up a winding gravel road filled with potholes and weeds towards a lone house on the very top of the mountain. It sat at the extreme edge of a cliff. At a glance, you could see the home was abandoned. It was unpainted, and the shutters were falling off. The front porch was rotting, and the door was broken.

The house was situated so that it completely obscured the view to the rear of the home. Due to the irregularly shaped cliff's edge, there was no way to walk around the house. Getting to the back of the home required walking through the house. Of course, this meant entering through the rickety front door.

You asked yourself why the agent brought you to this god-forsaken place as you crept up the unstable wooden steps. The broken front door squeaked as you eased it open just barely enough to enter the home. This house was clearly in horrible shape. Cobwebs and mice droppings were scattered throughout. Dust floated in the stale air. Peeling paint dripped from the walls.

As you walked to the back of the house, you were bewildered. A bright light gleamed from outside the back of the home. At the rear of the filthy living room, you saw a majestic door made of rich mahogany and a leaded glass window cut so perfectly it seemed to amplify the light passing through it. You stepped out of the shabby house through this beautiful door onto the back porch.

Unlike the front, the back porch was in perfect shape. Freshly painted wood was bright white. Two warm and inviting rocking chairs faced east, overlooking the cliff. A hint of evergreen was in the cool air. The view that was not visible from the front of the home was spectacular from the back porch. Gazing across the valley, the horizon stretched to eternity. The river below led to an impressive waterfall. Birds glided on the updrafts, and you could hear children laughing and church bells ringing. It was as if you looked over all of creation. In fact, in that instance, you wondered if you had caught a glimpse of God Himself. With no hesitation, you told the agent you would buy this house.

That was many years ago. Drawn by the perfect beauty of the back door and the brilliant light that streamed through it, you have spent years working on the main living spaces. You have painted, repaired, and arranged things so that guests may enjoy the view out from the back of the house and experience the light and the beauty and the awe. As time has passed, the evidence of your hard work is beginning to show.

Yet, the front of the house still looks dreadful. Guests still have to drive up that same old pock-filled road overgrown with weeds. The front door is still broken, and the landscaping neglected. You just have not taken the time to fix up the front because you know that what lies inside is far more important. That your guests have to enter through the broken door is somewhat discomforting; still, you know the beauty of what is in store for them inside and out-back.

Explanation of the Parable
Friends, we are the broken door! We are all in need of repair. Perhaps our door only needs the hinges oiled. Perhaps it needs to be planed down in order to fit the door frame now that the house has settled over the years. Perhaps it has some rotted-out spots in need of putty, sanding, and refinishing. No matter what it needs, it can be opened even in its broken condition.

The interior of the home is our heart, soul, and mind. These are the areas we first need to repair to make them appealing to the guests we invite inside.

Our guests are those people we encounter every day. Everyone we meet in all of the environments in which we live—at home, at work, and in our community—can see by our actions and our words what is in our hearts.

That magnificent, beautiful, and perfect back door is Jesus Christ our Savior. And the view from the back porch is the view of God. The only way we are able to get to God is through the door of Jesus Christ.

As I said, the glorious view is obscured completely unless one enters through the broken front door. Even though our door squeaks, has rotted spots, and is out of square, people can still enter into our home and experience the Christ in us. Upon entering, our guests will experience the warmth and love inside. They will quickly see that you have situated everything in your home around the streaming light of Jesus Christ and that Jesus is the door that leads to God.

Now comes the challenging part. We cannot, we must not, wait until the door is perfect before inviting others into our life to meet Jesus who dwells within us. That we need to work on our door is true. The weathering and deterioration of the door is the sin in our life. The rain of selfishness, the wind of worldly concerns will always beat on our door. But if we wait for perfection, we will deny others the opportunity to meet Jesus. And it is through Jesus that we bring others to God. Jesus calls us as we are, broken, to be the door through which others can enter to meet Him.

* * *

As a result of this parable, I felt prompted to found Broken Door Ministries. Through this ministry, I have been blessed to write about and speak on the subject of God's mercy and forgiveness and His clarion call to us, His broken people, to become a eucharistic people. I have discovered that it is through our response to this call that we can find healing in our own lives and bring about a similar healing in the lives of others.

With all of this as the backdrop and with the message of the *Parable of the Broken Door* as guiding inspiration, I will now endeavor to guide you through the process of becoming Eucharist for others. Our journey begins in the following chapter, with the simple title, **Blessed**. The title may be simple but internalizing and absorbing the meaning behind the title is a lifelong process.

BLESSED

GOD'S UNWARRANTED LOVE

> *"For I received from the Lord what I also handed on to you, that the Lord Jesus, on the night he was handed over, took bread, and, after he had given thanks, broke it and said, "This is my body that is for you. Do this in remembrance of me." In the same way also the cup, after supper, saying, "This cup is the new covenant in my blood. Do this, as often as you drink it, in remembrance of me." For as often as you eat this bread and drink the cup, you proclaim the death of the Lord until he comes."* 1 Corinthians 11:23-26

Just as Jesus blessed the bread and wine, He has blessed us as well. This is one of the shortest chapters, yet it contains the most important message—the timeless message of God's love for His people.

"What is the greatest blessing in your life?" what would your answer be? You might be inclined to answer your spouse, children, parents, food, shelter, health, or life itself. The reality is that we have so many blessings in our life that they can easily become overlooked or, worse yet, underappreciated. If, however, we are pressed to choose only one blessing as the greatest of all blessings, what would it be?

I believe there are two aspects of God's love that are so intrinsically intertwined that they actually become one blessing. Those blessings are **mercy** and **forgiveness**. Without God's mercy and forgiveness, all other blessings would be temporary and fading. As sinners, we have all fallen short of God's glory. But, at the core of our Christian faith is our understanding that our God has unconditional love for us. We believe that God sent His only Son to pay the price for our sins. Through His reparation on the cross, He restored us to the Father and opened wide the gates to eternal life.

We must never lose sight of the reality that God's mercy and forgiveness are gratuitously given to us. They are unwarranted by us, and we are completely undeserving of these blessings.

The incredible blessing of God's mercy and forgiveness are summed up in these few Bible passages.

God's Unwarranted Love
Romans 5:8: *But God proves his love for us in that while we were still sinners Christ died for us.*

He Seeks the Lost
Luke 19:10: *For the Son of Man has come to seek and to save what was lost.*

He Rejoices Over the Saved
Matthew 18:12-13: *"What is your opinion? If a man has a hundred sheep and one of them goes astray, will he not leave the ninety-nine in the hills and go in search of the stray? And if he finds it, amen, I say to you, he rejoices more over it than over the ninety-nine that did not stray."*

Jesus Gives Us Strength To Overcome Our Weaknesses
2 Corinthians 12:9: *And He has said to me, "My grace is sufficient for you, for power is perfected in weakness."*

He Wants Us To Have Eternal Life

John 3:16: *For God so loved the world that he gave his only Son, so that everyone who believes in him might not perish but might have eternal life.*

My dear friends, Christ longs to shine the light of His love and mercy in our hearts to illuminate those sins that prevent us from drawing closer to Him. His mercy is greater than our greatest sin and our darkest moments. In his book, *The Name Of God Is Mercy*, Pope Francis once stated, **"Only he who has been touched and caressed by the tenderness of His mercy really knows the Lord."**[4] Have you felt His soft touch and gentle caress?

Allow me to draw your attention to another passage from Pope Francis' book, *The Name of God Is Mercy*. In this book, Pope Francis refers to a story found in Bruce Marshall's novel, *To Every Man a Penny*.[5]

SOLDIER/PRIEST STORY

Gaston, a young priest, needs to hear the confession of a young German soldier whom the French have captured and have sentenced to death. The soldier admits his passion for a woman and the numerous amorous adventures he has had. He tells the priest that he is not sorry for all of this. The priest explains that he must repent in order to obtain forgiveness and absolution. "How can I repent? It was something I enjoyed, and if I had the chance, I would do it again."

Father Gaston wanted to absolve this man who was about to die. *"But are you sorry that you are not sorry,"* he asked.

The soldier thought for a moment and said, "Yes, I am sorry that I am not sorry." He knew he should be sorry, but for some reason, he just wasn't.

The young priest said, "That's all the opening God's mercy needs." And with that, he absolved the man's sins.

In this same book, Pope Francis states the following, "**God is crazy in love with us.**"[6]

Now for just a few moments, can you imagine that Jesus takes

His hand and places it over your head, and one drop of the blood that was shed on Calvary begins to wash over you. It covers your whole being. Jesus speaks these words to you, *"I forgive you!"* He continues by saying, *"I died on the cross to pay the price for your sins."* My friends, Jesus longs to forgive you. Will you let Him?

As we come to the end of this chapter, let's reflect on the father in the parable of the prodigal son. Here is the account from Luke 15:20, *'So he got up and went back to his father. While he was still a long way off, his father caught sight of him, and was filled with compassion.* ***He ran to his son****, embraced him and kissed him.'* I am always struck by the fact that the father ran to the son to embrace him even before the son had the opportunity to utter one word of his planned apology.

Like the father in the story, our Heavenly Father waits patiently and lovingly for us to become aware of our sins and turn away from them. He longs for us to return home to Him. When we do, He will run to embrace us, and He will pour out His mercy upon us.

MUSIC MEDITATION

I am a huge fan of music. Certain songs have a way of touching my soul. I will highlight several songs throughout this book to bring an emphasis to the message of the moment. I believe that if you listen to these songs, their powerful lyrics will help you retain the book's message.

For my first suggestion, I encourage you to download and listen to the song *"When God Ran"* by Phillips, Craig, and Dean. Allow the moving words to touch your soul. God is prepared to run out to us as soon as we repent and turn back to Him.

The song reminds us of how anxious God is to forgive us. In the story of the Prodigal Son, God ran out to his son as soon as he caught sight of him. God is ready to run to you right now. Will you let him?

Beyond a doubt, we are all enormously BLESSED. Amen!

BROKEN

BROKEN
BY SIN

> *"Jesus addressed this parable to those who were convinced of their own righteousness and despised everyone else. "Two people went up to the temple area to pray; one was a Pharisee and the other was a tax collector. The Pharisee took up his position and spoke this prayer to himself, 'O God, I thank you that I am not like the rest of humanity — greedy, dishonest, adulterous — or even like this tax collector. I fast twice a week, and I pay tithes on my whole income.' But the tax collector stood off at a distance and would not even raise his eyes to heaven but beat his breast and prayed, 'O God, be merciful to me a sinner.' I tell you, the latter went home justified, not the former; for everyone who exalts himself will be humbled, and the one who humbles himself will be exalted."* Luke 18:9-14

It is now time to shift away from the pleasant and reassuring discussion of God's mercy and forgiveness to the topic of our brokenness. I believe the passage above from Luke's Gospel is a good way to set the stage for the points I want to make in this chapter.

Just like the tax collector, we too, need to be able to acknowledge our broken condition. I have discovered that this can be hard for some people to do. In an effort to clarify just exactly what I mean by brokenness, I want to consider the term "broken" from two separate perspectives: broken and wounded. My hope is that by doing this, every one of us will be able to say, "Yes, I can see that I am broken too."

I personally believe that all of us are either broken by our own sins or we are wounded by the broken world in which we live. Many of us, if not all of us, if we are honest with ourselves, need to acknowledge that we are both broken and wounded.

Let's first dig a little deeper into this concept of being broken by our sin. What does the Bible have to tell us about all of this? Here are a few more verses.

Romans 3:23: *All have sinned and are deprived of the glory of God.*

Galatians 5:16-19, 22-23: *Let the Spirit direct your lives, and you will not satisfy the desires of human nature. For what is human nature is opposed to what the Spirit wants, and what the Spirit wants is opposed to what human nature wants. What human nature does is quite plain. It shows itself in immoral, filthy, and indecent actions. But the Spirit produces love, joy, peace, patience, kindness, goodness, faithfulness, humility, and self-control. The Spirit has given us life; he must also control our lives.*

Romans 7:14-15, 22-24: *We know that the Law is Spiritual: but I am a mortal, sold as a slave to sin. I do not understand what I do: for I don't do what I would like to do, but instead do what I hate. My inner being delights in the Law of God. But I see a different law at work in my body - a law that fights against the law which my mind approves of. It makes me a* **PRISONER** *to the law of sin, which is at work in my body.*

In his book, *The Lamb's Supper*, Catholic author Scott Hahn talks about our humanness this way, "We have an obligation, first to resist temptation. If we fail then and we sin, we have an obligation to repent immediately. If we do not repent, then God lets us have our way: He allows us to experience the natural consequences of our sins, the illicit pleasures. If we fail to repent through self-denial and acts of penance, God allows us to continue in sin, thereby forming a habit, a vice, **which darkens our intellect and weakens our wills.**"[7]

Pope Francis weighed in on the topic of brokenness with this quote, "The church is a field hospital for the wounded in a cruel world."[8]

All of the above Bible verses and quotes make it clear that we all must contend with our sinful nature. Sin has been part of the human experience since the beginning of mankind. Take a look at this dialog from Genesis 3:

God said, *"From that tree you shall not eat; the moment you eat from it you are surely doomed to die."*

Satan, in the form of a serpent, says, *"Did God really say, 'You shall not eat from any of the trees in the garden'?"*

Then he continued by saying, *"You certainly will **not** die!"*

We all know what happened next. The story tells us that Adam and Eve ate from the forbidden tree. Satan lied to them to get them to sin, and Satan has been lying and deceiving us ever since!

In fact, the Bible tells us that evil is inside of each of us, *"But what comes out of the man, that is what defiles him. From within the man, from his heart, come evil thoughts, unchastity, theft, murder, adultery, greed, malice, deceit, licentiousness, envy, blasphemy, arrogance, folly. All these evils come from within and they defile."* (Mark 7:14-23)

Sadly, this evil raises its ugly head from time to time. Sadder yet is the reality that most of us have one or two sins that seem to be like a ball and chain around our ankle. We tend to return to those same sins over and over again. It seems that no matter how many times we turn to God and confess our sin, we eventually commit these same sins again. For many people, this develops into a repetitive pattern of sinning, confessing, and then sinning again.

Repentance is a start. It is clearly important. Repentance was the message that was preached by both John the Baptist and Jesus. Let's take a closer look at what they said.

We read in Matthew 3:1-2, *"In those days John the Baptist appeared, preaching in the desert of Judea [and] saying, "Repent, for the kingdom of heaven is at hand!"* Mark 1:4 presents it this way, *"John [the] Baptist appeared in the desert proclaiming a baptism of repentance for the forgiveness of sins."* Finally, in Acts 13:24, we see the same message, *"John heralded his coming by proclaiming a baptism of repentance to all the people of Israel."*

As Jesus began His public ministry following His time in the desert, He continued with the same message of repentance that John had preached. In Matthew 4:17, this is written, *"From that time on, Jesus began to preach and say, 'Repent, for the kingdom of heaven is at hand.'"* But here is a very important point. Jesus added a few additional requirements—we must do more than just repent. Take a look.

Jesus told us that His message was for the sick, not the healthy. He told us that we needed to believe in the Gospel. He told us we need to be converted so that our sins can be wiped away. In other words, we need to change our ways. And finally, He challenged us through the message He gave the woman caught in adultery when He says, *"Go and sin no more."* (John 8:11)

Luke 5:31-32: *Jesus said to them in reply, "Those who are healthy do not need a physician,* **but the sick do***. I have not come to call the righteous to repentance but sinners."*

Mark 1:15: *"This is the time of fulfillment. The kingdom of God is at hand. Repent, and **believe in the gospel**."*

Acts 3:19: *"Repent, therefore, and **be converted**, that your sins may be wiped away."*

John 8:10-11: *Then Jesus straightened up and said to her, "Woman, where are they? Has no one condemned you?" She replied, "No one, sir." Then Jesus said, "Neither do I condemn you. Go, [and] from now on **do not sin any more**."*

I believe it is safe to say that we are much better at repenting than we are at being changed and converted. We're sorry, yet we don't let go of our recurring sin, like the ghost in C. S. Lewis's story couldn't seem to get rid of the lizard. Change is hard, and we feel more comfortable stuck in our recurring patterns of brokenness. Why is this? Is there anything that can help us break this cycle? As the following chapters unfold, I will try to show you a path to healing and recovery from your nagging, recurring sins.

As I wrote earlier, Satan is a liar. In Genesis, Satan told Eve, *"Surely you will not die"*—but that is a lie. Each time we return to our sinful habits, we die a little inside. It has been said that sin is not just a stain. When we stain our clothes, we can take them to the dry cleaner. When we pick them up, the stain has been completely washed away. Clearly, Jesus forgives our sins when we repent, but unlike those clothes that we took to the dry cleaner, even after our sins have been forgiven, they leave lasting damage. Sin is better compared to a wound. After a wound heals, there is usually a scar left behind. Even after we know God has forgiven us, the scar from our sin remains. Those scars can take many years, if not a lifetime, to completely heal. We are sometimes haunted by our past sins, even though we know and trust that God is merciful and forgiving.

We see a strong parallel to this in the resurrected body of our Lord. When He is with the apostles, Jesus shows them the wounds of His crucifixion. Present in this miracle of His resurrected and life-affirming body is the retention of the wounds of our sins that He carries with him. In His healing presence, He shows us His wounds—which are also our wounds. They have become part of him, but they are also part of the miracle of His resurrection.

There is something positive that can result from having sinned and having been forgiven. It is in and through our sin and our subsequent repentance that we can come face to face with the mercy of our Lord Jesus Christ. When this happens, we can learn from our mistakes and draw closer to God as we journey onward.

Let me share another story. It relates to my involvement in Cursillo. Cursillo is a lay movement where one attends a three-day retreat and then plugs into a small group that meets weekly to discuss their daily walk with God. These groups gather once a month in what is known as Ultreya. My wife and I were the coordinators of Ultreya for our parish. We were getting discouraged because of low attendance. I remember back in the spring of 2011 asking my pastor for advice. Little did I know how positive an impact his answer would have on my life.

"Father Nick," I said. "Why do so many people make these Cursillo weekends and, while they are there, commit to God that they will attend these monthly gatherings for the rest of their life and then not do so?"

He answered, "That is a great question. Give me some time to pray over the answer, and I will get back with you."

It was about ten days later when Fr. Nick called and invited me to meet him at his office. On the day I went to visit with him, I sat directly across the desk from him as we had our conversation.

He said, "Brian, I have prayed over and given a lot of thought to your question."

He continued, "What you need to know is that every person is chained to some area of sin in their life. Some people are fortunate in that they know what their sin is. Other people live life, and they don't acknowledge their sins and offenses against God. They seem oblivious to or unaware of their sinfulness. I tell you this because when people give the excuse that they cannot attend the Ultreya because it is on a specific day of the week or a specific time of day that doesn't work for them, it is rarely the day or the time that is the real reason they don't show up. It is the sin in their life that pulls them away. It is the allure of something else that tells them this meeting is not as important as something else on their schedule."

He went on to say, "If you are going to be effective in leading this group and effective in evangelization, then you must understand the influence that sin has in each person's life."

It is what he said and did next that left a permanent impact on my life. He picked up a book from his desk, and he handed it to me as he said, "Brian, what you must also understand is that you, too, have your own areas of sin and brokenness that impact your life. **Until you come to grips with your own brokenness, you will never be as effective at evangelizing others as God intends for you to be.**"

Wow! In that moment, I felt as if he had read my soul. I, unconsciously and instinctively, leaned back in my chair and crossed my arms over my chest as if to protect myself. Did he know about my lizard? He may remember some of the sins I've confessed, but somehow, I felt as if he was aware of all of my hidden faults and shortcomings.

The book he gave me was, *Unbound* by Neal Lozano. He suggested that this book would help me better understand the ball and chain of my own recurring sin.

This conversation caught me by surprise. It led me in a totally different direction than I anticipated when I asked the simple question, "Why don't people attend Ultreya?"

Fr. Nick gave me some additional advice. He asked me if I had ever been on a silent retreat. I told him that I had not. He then suggested that I make that eight-day silent retreat that I've mentioned earlier. I did so just two months later, in November of 2011. It was on that retreat that I finally finished *Unbound*.

This retreat left an indelible imprint on my life. I've already written a lot about my experience while in the retreat, and I will write much more about its impact on my life later in the book. For now, the main message I want to convey to you is the message that Fr. Nick conveyed to me. We all have some area of sin in our life that chains us down. We are broken by our own sinfulness. It may not be necessary for everyone to go on a silent retreat to have a life-changing revelation, but it is critically important that we all find quiet time to be alone with God so that He can reveal the sins in our life that offend Him.

In summary, we are responsible for the brokenness in our life because it is caused by our sins. As Paul states, this evil comes from within us.

The wounds in our life, however, are inflicted upon us from outside. They are not our fault. These wounds come about because we live in a broken world. Our wounds can also be caused by the sins of others. We will discover more about our wounds in the next chapter.

WOUNDED BY THE WORLD

The righteous cry out, the LORD hears and he rescues them from all their afflictions. The LORD is close to the brokenhearted, saves those whose spirit is crushed. —Psalm 34: 19-19

In the retreats that I lead in churches around the country, I make this statement, "Perhaps the two most philosophical and theological words ever conjoined by the mind of man were combined on a bumper sticker in the 1980s, and those two words were **STUFF HAPPENS**, except on the bumper sticker the word wasn't *stuff*. Everyone knows what I mean, and my statement usually gets a laugh from the crowd.

According to Wikipedia, the term *"Stuff Happens"* (the less vulgar way to say it) is used as a simple existential observation that life is full of unpredictable events. The phrase is an acknowledgment that bad things happen to people seemingly for no particular reason. First observed in 1964, this phrase wasn't used in a print publication until 1983.

This begs the question. When bad things happen to people, is God responsible for causing them to happen?

Recently there was heavy rain in the area where I live. Two news reporters were covering a story where a mudslide had occurred. While still sitting in their work vehicle, a tree fell on their car, killing both men. Did God make this happen?

We often hear stories about tornadoes going through a town causing widespread destruction. Sometimes people are killed on one side of the street while their neighbors across the street sustain little or no damage. Does God cause the tornado to kill only specific people?

During the summer months, the news brings sad stories about young children who drown in swimming pools, lakes, and ponds. Does God single out these children and cause them to fall in the water?

Some children are sexually abused by parents, family members, neighbors, or trusted people in authority. Does God purposely cause or allow these tragic acts to occur?

Some people develop serious illnesses and suffer and die as a result of these illnesses, while other people live long, healthy lives. Does God like some people more than others?

Some babies are born with birth defects, while others are born healthy. Is God purposely picking on these children and their parents?

Some people are suddenly and without notice killed in car accidents. Does God cause this to happen?

Some people end up in abusive marriages. Is this by God's design?

Some people develop addictions to drugs, alcohol, pain medicines, pornography, and unwanted sexual behaviors. Does God make some people more susceptible to addiction than others?

Some Christians during their adolescence discover that they are attracted to their same sex. For those who discover they are same-sex attracted, life can be a trial. Did God make some people same-sex attracted only to tell them they could not act on those attractions as some type of mystical punishment?

The list of questions I could ask goes on and on. I think you get my point. Now allow me to offer my thoughts on these questions. It is my strongly held belief that the answer to all of the questions above is a resounding NO!

God created a perfect world. According to Genesis, God created a world where men did not have to work, and women did not experience labor pains when giving birth. What changed this? Sin changed it. After original sin entered the world, all kinds of bad things began to happen. The world as the creator designed it changed. God does not want to see us suffer. He wants us to be happy. But bad things do happen.

I believe that God cries when we cry. Jesus cried at the death of His friend Lazarus. I believe God is saddened when we are saddened. When pain and suffering befall us, God hurts for us. In other words, we live in a broken and fractured world, a world vastly different from the Garden of Eden. To sum this up, we live in a world where STUFF HAPPENS!

When STUFF HAPPENS, and when people suffer, they sometimes blame God for their pain and loss. Their wounds can become a barrier or impediment in their relationship with God.

Hopefully, I have made the point that our own sinful behavior causes our brokenness, and living in a broken and imperfect world causes our wounds. In either case, our brokenness and wounds can fracture our relationship with God.

We will see in the next chapter how our PRIDE can get in the way of our healing and recovery. As I bring this chapter to a close, I hope that we can agree that all of us are broken or wounded in some way.

MUSIC MEDITATION

I want to encourage you to take a moment to download and listen to the song *"Broken"* by Kenneth Cope. This song has become my adopted theme song for Broken Door Ministries. It has helped me to focus on the reality that God knows I am a broken person, and He loves me anyhow. It also points out that God has a long history of using broken things for good.

He wants to use you too, despite any brokenness you might have, to bring glory to His Kingdom. Will you let Him?

The fact is we are all BROKEN. Amen.

SCARED

MASKS

> *"Do not fear, for I have redeemed you;*
> *I have called you by name: you are mine."*
> Isaiah 43:1

Have you seen the play *Phantom of the Opera*? The curtain opens for the second act with a large group of people standing on a grand staircase. Each person is wearing a colorful costume and a mask. The song that accompanies this scene is "Masquerade," by Andrew Lloyd Weber, and it brings to life the reality that we are surrounded by people wearing masks. As long as people have their masks on, it is difficult to know the true identity hidden by the mask.

If I were to meet you face to face and I was wearing a Phantom Mask, could you listen to what I have to say and take what I say seriously? Probably not. With that said, can and should anyone you meet, take you and what you have to say seriously? Be honest, aren't you wearing a mask right now? I believe that most, if not all, people wear a mask throughout much of their life.

People typically wear masks because they are scared. They fear having others see them as they really are. Sometimes we are even scared to see ourselves as we really are. In just a moment, I will describe three types of distinct masks that I have identified. But before I do, I want to dig deeper into the word *scared*.

Focus on the **C** in scared for a moment. When you see the C in the word scared, I want you to think of the word *CHAGRIN*. Two words used to define *chagrin* are humiliation and embarrassment. Perhaps these two words sum up the reason why we are scared. We often torture ourselves by telling ourselves this, "If someone knew the real me, the one with all of my faults, sins, and failures, no one would like me. I might lose my friends or my spouse or my family."

With this fear firmly in place, we wear masks to make everyone think our life is "fine." After all, isn't that what we say to someone when they ask us how we are? Think about that for a minute. How do you answer the question, "How are you?" Our reactive answer is, "Fine—I'm fine."

If we want to live honestly, we need to have a **transparent personality**. We need to take our masks off. Jesus came to save the lost and broken—why do we want to pretend we are not broken?

The answer to that question is simple. The answer is Satan. Satan causes us to live in a world of delusion, unreality, and shadows. He is the great illusionist. He varnishes the truth and encourages our dishonesty. The end result is this—we put on our masks.

As I said, I have identified three unique types of masks that people wear. As I describe each one separately, you might come to realize which one you are wearing. You might even realize that you are wearing more than one.

MASK ONE: *Hiding ourselves from others.*

Do you have sins and wounds in your life that no one is aware of but you? Do you prefer to keep these struggles hidden? Are you afraid of how others would react if they knew you had these imperfections? For some reason, we try to convince ourselves that no one would love us if they really knew us. Rest assured, God knows us better than anyone, and He still loves us. Maybe others would, too. In fact, maybe if they knew us with all of our shortcomings, they might actually like and respect us even more.

The song *"Stained Glass Masquerade"* by Casting Crowns speaks to this issue of being afraid. This song reminds the listener that although they may feel like they are the only broken and sinful person in church, it is simply not true. Everyone in the church is broken. Unfortunately, everyone hides their brokenness behind the allusion that they are fine. In the end, mask-wearing hurts everyone. Each person feels isolated and alone, and they often feel like they don't belong in this large group of "saintly perfect people."

Recognizing your own faults and sins, have you ever sat in church feeling this way? Have you sat in your pew keenly aware of your brokenness while at the same time thinking that everyone sitting around you has it all together? Trust me, they don't. They just know how to wear their masks as well as you know how to wear yours.

MASK TWO: *Hiding ourselves from ourselves.*
Mask Two can be much worse than Mask One. Do you dislike your personal flaws so much that you just pretend they don't exist? Self-deception prevents us from seeing ourselves as we really are. If we are not honest with ourselves, how can we expect to change? How can we expect to overcome our flaws if we won't acknowledge them?

Pope Francis was once asked this question, "What would you say to someone who doesn't feel like a sinner?" His answer speaks directly to this issue of self-deception. He said, **"I would advise him to ask for the grace of feeling like one."**

Permit me to share a funny story with you.

There was a very self-righteous man who went to his doctor complaining of a sharp shooting pain in his head. During the exam, the doctor asked the man to show him exactly where the pain was located. The man pointed all the way around his head. Finding no medical cause for the pain, the doctor told the man that he had discovered the problem. The man asked, "What is it, Doc?" The doctor replied, "I think you have your halo on too tight. Maybe you need to loosen it up a bit."

Are you wearing your halo too tight?

Have you had your mask on so long that you no longer recognize yourself?

The Sin of Pride is considered by some to be the foremost of the Seven Deadly Sins. Satan uses our pride, and he uses shame to wall us in. With Mask One, we become keenly aware of our own faults, and we tend to look at everyone else as if they have none. Fearful of what others would think if they knew us as we truly are, we carefully secure our masks in place. With Mask Two, we simply fail to accept that we have faults. With either mask in place, we remain stuck behind the walls of shame and pride. As long as we hide and remain silent about our brokenness, our efforts to overcome our brokenness will fail over and over again. We will remain captive to our brokenness, and these sins will recur throughout our life.

Our hidden wounds and our hidden brokenness brought about by our recurring sins work together to enslave us. If we hope to find freedom from our brokenness, we must eventually overcome our pride and shame and become vulnerable. I will talk more about this later in the book.

Mask Three is uniquely different than Masks One and Two. With Mask One, we deceive others, and with Mask Two, we deceive ourselves. With Mask Three, Satan tries to deceive us.

MASK THREE: *Having our real brokenness hidden from us by Satan.*
How does Satan do this? By making us focus ***only*** on what we wrote down on our Purple Paper. If you are wearing Mask One, you may be overly focused on your recurring sin and blind to some other area of sin in your life that is far more offensive to God. If you are wearing Mask Two, you must first take off your mask and acknowledge that you have recurring sinfulness in your life. Once you do that, you must be as careful as the person who was wearing Mask One to not allow Satan to deceive you. Those sins that recur on a frequent basis in your life may be a subterfuge so that you miss other areas of sin that should demand your immediate attention.

Earlier with the Purple Paper exercise, you wrote down on side one the areas of wounds in your life, and on side two, you wrote down the recurring sin which you are most aware of. Now, I want to walk you through a **yellow paper exercise.**

EXERCISE TWO

THE YELLOW PAPER EXERCISE

Please find a 3-by-5-inch index card and write the words Yellow Paper Exercise on it. There is also a card on the last page of the book that you can cut out and use for this exercise.

```
┌─────────────────────────────┐
│        Yellow Paper         │
│                             │
│                             │
└─────────────────────────────┘
```

On side one, draw a large question mark that takes up the entire side of the paper. On side two, write down this translation of Psalm 139:23-24:

Search me O God and know my heart, test me and know my anxious thoughts, point out anything in me that offends you, and lead me on the path to everlasting life.

The question to focus on is this: Is the recurring sin that you regularly confess the *real sin* that actually separates you from a fuller relationship with God, or is it a distraction coming from Satan? Does Satan have you focused on the wrong thing?

As examples of this, perhaps you have gossip written down on your Purple Paper, and you confess that sin repeatedly, but hidden by that sin is the bigger sin of envy that you fail to confess. Perhaps you struggle with a porn viewing addiction and have that written on your Purple Paper and you constantly confess it but hidden by it is your sin of pride which you never confess. Finally, perhaps Satan keeps your focus solely on your sins of commission and you never seek forgiveness for any sins of omission. Do you ever confess the sins of not visiting those in prison or those who are sick in the hospital?

Commit yourself to 30 days of prayer over your yellow paper. Recite the Psalm during your prayer. Beg God to reveal anything in you that is offensive to Him. You might be surprised to discover that you have been focused on the wrong thing for way too long. This does not mean that you do not need to work to overcome those things listed on your Purple Paper. No, it means that there are bigger areas of brokenness and/or sinfulness that you are completely overlooking that need serious attention.

All three of these masks take us back to where we began. We are scared. We are frightened. We are afraid we might be humiliated or embarrassed if others knew us in our broken condition. What are we all afraid of? The Bible is very clear on this point: **WE ALL NEED TO BE SAVED!** We cannot save ourselves. Try as we may, we will only fail.

Permit me to use a joke to make my point.

There was a salesman going downtown to the most important and largest sales call he had ever been on. When he arrived downtown for his appointment, there were no parking spaces. Acting quickly, he looked up to the heavens and said, "God, if you will help me find a parking space, I will start going to church every Sunday and further, God, if you help me find this parking space, I will give up drinking alcohol for the rest of my life." Just then, miraculously, a parking space became available. The man then looked back up to the heavens and said, "Never mind, God, I found one all on my own."

The humor contained in this joke illustrates a very important point. We cannot save ourselves! We need God!

In 1 Timothy 1:15, Paul writes, *"Of all sinners, I am the worst!"* But Paul also gives us this encouragement in Romans 7:24-25, *"Miserable one that I am! Who will deliver me from this mortal body? Thanks be to God through Jesus Christ our Lord."*

Paul affirms the struggles that we all have. All of us battle sin and temptation in our lives. Struggles are real, and for some of us, they are debilitating.

Pope Francis offers us this wisdom, "The repentant sinner, who sins again and again because of his weakness, will find forgiveness if he acknowledges his need for mercy."[9]

Healing is available for us if only we take a small step toward God. It first begins by just desiring to take that step. To be effective in evangelization, we must remove our masks! How are you doing with that?

I firmly believe that one of the reasons we are seeing a drop in the number of Christians who attend church on Sundays is because our modern culture has told us that, "I'm okay, and you're okay just the way we are." In essence, we don't acknowledge our need for mercy. The truth is we are not okay. We are broken. And even so, God loves us just as we are. He loves us no matter what. He loves us even in our brokenness. And He loves us so much that He doesn't want us to stay as we are. He is there to forgive us and lend us a guiding hand back to the path of truth. If, as our culture tries to tell us, we are all okay as we are, then we have no need to be saved. If we have no need to be saved, then we have no need for a savior. If we have no need for a savior, then Jesus died in vain, and certainly, there would be no need to go to church on Sundays.

The church is a gathering place for sinners. Therefore, we must first accept the fact that we are sinners in need of being saved to understand the importance of setting aside Sunday to be with our Savior.

Healing is available for us if only we take a small step toward God. It first begins by just desiring to take that step. And to be effective in evangelization, we must remove our masks! How are you doing with that?

If you are reading this book and you either don't feel broken or don't clearly see the areas of sinfulness in your life, I offer you the following spiritual tools:

Time for God
Consider, if possible, making time to get away on a silent retreat. Give God the time and space to talk to you and give yourself the ideal condition to hear Him. If getting away is not possible, then try setting aside fifteen minutes of silence each morning so that God can speak to you to reveal areas in your life that need some improvement.

Spiritual Direction

If you currently do not have a Spiritual Director, I strongly encourage you to find one. Having a trained Spiritual Director can be very beneficial. Sometimes we are simply unable to see things about ourselves or our spiritual journey that someone who is trained in spiritual direction can see.

Fasting

Finally, I also want to encourage you to fast as a regular part of your Christian Life. Fasting was an expected discipline used in both the Old and New Testaments. In the book of Acts 14:23, we find this, *"They appointed presbyters for them in each church and, with prayer and fasting, commended them to the Lord in whom they had put their faith."* Sadly, for many Christians, the tradition of fasting has been relegated to something done only during Lent if done at all.

Using these three spiritual tools of retreats, spiritual direction, and fasting can be very helpful when undertaking a personal spiritual analysis. We might discover that God has a lot to say. He sure had a lot to say to me when I made a retreat.

THE ENCOUNTER WITH GOD THAT CHANGED MY LIFE!

As I previously mentioned, it was in November of 2011 that I attended the eight-day retreat in Clearwater, Florida. I believe now that my experience on this Ignatian retreat was nothing short of miraculous-

On the second night of that retreat, I was struck by an overwhelming feeling that Mary, the Mother of Our Lord, directed Fr. Nick to give me the book, *Unbound*, and she guided him to recommend that I make this retreat, specifically so that I could have a very personal encounter with her Son. I personally believe that any time Mary intercedes on our behalf, it is always for the express purpose of directing our focus towards her Son Jesus.

It was, however, during the third night of the retreat, while I was kneeling in prayer in the chapel, that my life was dramatically changed. In the silent dimness, I suddenly felt God speaking directly to my heart. This is what I heard Him say, *"Brian, if you want to heal, you have to tell someone you are broken."* I knew in an instant what this message meant. I began to cry.

For over 42 years, I harbored a deep and dark secret. There was only one person in my life who knew of this secret, and that was my wife. God was calling me to confront this brokenness in my life. You see, when I was a young Altar Server, I had been sexually molested by a Catholic priest in my parish.

I never found the courage to tell anyone what happened to me. I did not tell my parents, nor did I tell my brother. It remained my hidden secret. I had no idea back then that this event would impact the rest of my life.

Earlier in the book, when explaining the Purple Paper Exercise, I put forth the idea that brokenness took two forms. We are all *broken* by our own sins. Many of us are also *wounded* by the sins of others or by simply living in a broken world. There was no doubt that this man's sins left me with lasting wounds.

There has been a lot written in the news about the priest abuse scandal recently. While I am no expert on this topic, I can tell you that I know far more about it than I ever wanted to know. Childhood sexual abuse and molestation take many forms. Child sexual abuse is not limited to Catholic priests. Many children are molested at the hands of parents, stepparents, other family members, ministers, teachers, and other people in authority.

Some, but not all, are physically harmed by the abuse. I was not. I am convinced, however, that all victims are psychologically harmed. The psychological harm manifests itself in as many different ways are there are children who have been abused.

One of the most common impacts of abuse is **shame**. Victims often place some or all of the blame on themselves. This is especially true if the molestation and/or abuse results in the victim experiencing some sexual pleasure as a result of what is being done to them. This was the case for me. It is still hard for me to believe that I just wrote this down in this book. It is still painful for me to admit that. This is the reason that I never had the courage to tell anyone other than my wife.

Another harmful effect of having been abused is to end up with a distorted view of normal, healthy human sexuality. Many victims struggle with sexual issues and addictions following the abuse. These issues can remain with the victims for years and sometimes for a lifetime. I must admit that after the abuse, I frequently struggled with the sin of lust and with the virtue of chastity.

The rush of postpubescent hormones coupled with the lingering memory of the molestation created quite a struggle for me during my formative years. My teenage years hardwired my young brain through the process that psychologists call *adolescent brain mapping*. My quest for sexual purity seemed elusive. Lust became the frequently occurring topic of my all too regular trips to the sacrament of reconciliation (confession). I spent years fighting to break free from the chains of my broken childhood.

Lust and lack of chastity are the items written on my Purple Paper. These were my recurring sins. These were the things that I seemed to confess over and over again for years in the confessional. These were the sins that kept me chained down. Many psychologists have told me that this is normal for people who have experienced sexual abuse as a child. While this may be true, I still must take ownership of these sins and seek God's forgiveness. I can also assure you that Satan was using my weakness and my recurring sins, written down on my Purple Paper, to keep me from seeing many other sins that have subsequently been revealed by my Yellow Paper that were also damaging my relationship with God.

Now let's go back to the retreat. Here I was, kneeling in prayer on that third night when God told me that I needed to reveal these secrets if I wanted to be healed. Coming away from the retreat, I also felt the need to completely forgive the priest who had abused me. Although he had long ago passed away, I did, in fact, forgive him. I now pray for his soul to be saved.

There is no doubt that, while child sexual abuse is a heinous crime and a very serious sin, God's grace and mercy are greater than any sin. We are all sinners. This priest, too, was a sinner. The Lord's Prayer leads me to ask God to forgive my trespasses as I forgive those who trespass against me. I knew if I wanted forgiveness for my own sins, I also had to forgive. I am happy to say that I have forgiven the priest who abused me. God can forgive all sins, yes, even the sins of those who sexually abuse children. Assuming this priest sought God's forgiveness, I will likely see him in Heaven one day.

Both the abuse itself and my own struggles with lust and living chastely clouded my relationship with God. Shame had kept me silent for years. After all, when is the right time to tell your buddies that another man sexually molested you? And how many of us would willingly confess to our friends that we live unchastely and struggle with lust? Adding to my desire to remain silent was the false belief that I was the only one with these types of sin in my life. The fact is this: As long as we remain silent about our sins, we remain **captive** and **chained** to these sins. In 2011, I had been in a weekly prayer group with other men who were my closest Christian friends, yet even with these close friends, I could not muster the strength to discuss my brokenness with them. All of that changed after my silent retreat.

You have heard enough about my brokenness. You now know what is written on both sides of my Purple Paper. At this time, I want to borrow a technique from Jesus. We know that when Jesus begins a comment with, *"Amen, amen, I say to you,"* He is about to say something that is very important. In fact, I have been told we should write down the things He says after using this emphatic expression.

Now it is my turn to use those words. AMEN, AMEN I SAY TO YOU, this book is *not* about what is written on my Purple Paper. What matters is **WHAT'S WRITTEN ON YOUR PURPLE PAPER!** So now, let me ask you again this very important question, **"Does anyone else, besides perhaps your confessor, know what is written on your Purple Paper?"** Is your brokenness your best-kept secret? Mine was for over 42 years. God told me that if I wanted to heal, I had to make my brokenness known. Is God, right now through this book, telling you the same thing?

My life was forever changed on that retreat. After that retreat, I began to reveal my brokenness. I started slowly at first. I will write more about this later. It should be obvious to you now that by writing this book, I am shouting the story of my brokenness and the story of God's mercy and the resulting freedom I received from the mountaintops.

It was also after my encounter on that retreat that I felt called to start Broken Door Ministries and to begin writing *4th Day Letters*. It is very common throughout Christian history to be called into action after having a personal encounter with God. I have dedicated the balance of my life to helping others who are hurting, broken, and alone. I prayerfully hope that this book is helping you right now.

SUMMARY OF BEING SCARED

Not everyone who opens up about their brokenness will be called to start a ministry, but by opening up with someone, the healing process can begin. You will also be in a better position to help others with their brokenness after revealing and coming to grips with your own.

Let me try to provide a summary of this chapter on being scared. It is important to remember this: Humiliation, embarrassment, fear, and shame work to keep us behind our masks.

Clearly, not everyone is broken in the same way I was. **What is your brokenness**? Perhaps your brokenness takes the form of anger, control, envy, family strife, lying, the inability to forgive, pride, gossip, or some other sin.

We must all learn that we need to be transparent. Open, honest sharing is healthy for us. This is why the small Cursillo-like groups that meet weekly are so important. We need strong Christian friends who we trust and with whom we can share. We cannot let fear and shame stop us. Someone once told a speaker at a Catholic retreat that they could not possibly reveal their sins to a priest in the confessional. They said their sins were too embarrassing. That speaker jokingly replied by saying, "Get over yourself—your sins are just not that original."

Perhaps you are old enough to remember comedian George Carlin's seven dirty words that couldn't be said on television. It seems that for many of us, we have developed our own list of "dirty sins" or areas of personal brokenness that we can't admit anywhere or to anyone.

We must always remember that a scared Christian is an ineffective evangelizer. As Christians, we often hear the term **The Good News.** Just what is the good news? For me, the good news is this: We are broken, but Jesus loves us anyhow. It seems our God loves broken people. In fact, He loves us so much that He sent His Son to die on a cross so that He could save us from our brokenness. Our world is starving to hear this good news.

Ever since my retreat, there has been a Christian song, *"Hosea,"* written by John Michael Talbot, that really speaks to the point I am trying to make in this chapter. This song helps me to keep in mind that God is always calling me back. He is relentless in His pursuit of me. When I listen to the music, I am convicted with the understanding that I cannot allow fear to separate me from God. He has waited a long time for me, and he is waiting for you to come home to Him.

At this juncture in the book, can I get a big resounding amen to the fact that we are all blessed, broken, and **SCARED!**

At the beginning of this book, I said that I chose to name this book *Blessed, Broken, and Scared* because this is where many of us are stuck. I went on to say that if we are to become communion for others, we must go through a conversion to become a Blessed, Broken, and **SHARED** people. It is through sharing our brokenness and the story of God's forgiveness that we can finally become the eucharistic people we are called to be. "Shared" is the title of the next chapter.

MUSIC MEDITATION

I want to encourage you to take a moment to download and listen to the song *"Truth Be Told"* by Matthew West. This song has touched the core of my being.

It truly captures the human experience of trying to hide our brokenness. We always want to tell people we are fine, even when it is not true. What would happen if we opened up and told the truth? I feel certain this song with touch your heart too.

SHARED

OUR CALL
TO BE EUCHARIST

> *"While they were eating, Jesus took bread, said the blessing, broke it, and giving it to his disciples said, "Take and eat; this is my body." Then he took a cup, gave thanks, and gave it to them, saying, "Drink from it, all of you, for this is my blood of the covenant, which will be shed on behalf of many for the forgiveness of sins. I tell you, from now on I shall not drink this fruit of the vine until the day when I drink it with you new in the kingdom of my Father." Then, after singing a hymn, they went out to the Mount of Olives." — Matthew 26: 26-30*

The last meal that Jesus shared with His disciples is described in all four Gospels (Matthew 26:17-30, Mark 14:12-26, Luke 22:7-39, and John 13:1-17:26). This meal later became known as the Last Supper.

Take a closer look at the four things Jesus did to the bread during the last supper. He took it (in other words, He chose it), He blessed it, He broke it, and He **shared** it. Sharing is what this chapter is all about.

At the conclusion of the last chapter, we were still blessed, broken, and scared! But, this is not what we are called to be. We are called and chosen to be Eucharist: Blessed, Broken, and

SHARED! Blessed, broken, and SCARED is *not* Eucharist, Communion, nor is it the Lord's Supper. It is simply blessed and broken. *Scared* leaves us as ineffective evangelizers and keeps us broken.

Recall in the last chapter, I asked you to focus on the letter "C" in the word SCARED. The "C" represented the word chagrin. Now let's look at the word SHARED for just a minute. Focus on the H in shared. I want to put forth the notion that the H in shared stands for HONESTY. Honesty is defined as truthfulness, candor, or sincerity. If we are going to be honest, we must learn to admit our brokenness and become vulnerable. Think about how closely the words "SCARED" and "SHARED" are in spelling. There is only a one letter difference—a "C" and an "H." But oh, what a difference it is. The word scared carries the humiliation and embarrassment of chagrin, while the word shared carries the profound power of honesty. And contained within this honesty is the truth that will set you free.

I believe that the teachings of Christianity are clear. We are called to be Eucharist for others. Have you ever thought of yourself as EUCHARIST? Have you ever thought of yourself as communion for others? Have you ever thought that your calling as a Christian invites you to become spiritually part of the events of the Last Supper? Starting now, I hope I can convince you to begin thinking of yourself in this way.

Let's take a look at the story of the leper from Mark 1:40-45.

A leper came to him and, kneeling down, begged him and said, "If you wish, you can make me clean." Moved with pity, he stretched out his hand, touched him, and said to him, "I do will it. Be made clean." The leprosy left him immediately, and he was made clean. Then, warning him sternly, he dismissed him at once. Then he said to him, "See that you tell no one anything, but go, show yourself to the priest and offer for your cleansing what Moses prescribed; that will be proof for them." The man went away and began to publicize the whole matter. He spread the report abroad so that it was impossible for Jesus to enter a town openly. He remained outside in deserted places, and people kept coming to him from everywhere.

What do we see in this story? What I see is a man who was so overflowing with joy at being saved that he could not contain himself. He felt compelled to share his good news with others.

There is always joy in being saved. There is always awe in a personal encounter with Jesus. We cannot contain it. We must share it. Some will shout it from the mountain tops. Others will show it in quieter ways. But we all, like the leper, will be changed and want to share this good news in some way.

Sharing requires more than one person. We can't share with ourselves. Christianity is not a solo sport. By God's design, we are communal people. Christian Community is essential if we are going to be disciples of Jesus Christ. This reminds me of the Three Dog Night song, "One Is The Loneliest Number." Mother Teresa once said, "Loneliness is the most terrible poverty." Perhaps author Dietrich Bonhoeffer said it best when he said, "He who is alone with his sins is utterly alone!"[10]

True Christian friendship is an essential part of the journey of life. One of my favorite writings on the importance of friendship comes from the book Sirach (also known as Ecclesiasticus). This book, with its ethical teachings, comes from a period approximately 200 to 175 years before Christ. This book is contained in Catholic Bibles and some Episcopal or Lutheran Bibles. While it is not contained in the primary text of a Protestant Bible, it is usually contained in the addendum known as the apocryphal books. This is neither the time nor place to discuss the merits of this book as to its divine inspiration. The fact remains that the wisdom contained in this book on the subject of friendship is just as sound today for all people as it was at the time it was written. Here is what is written in Sirach 6:14-16:

"Faithful friends are a sturdy shelter; whoever finds one finds a treasure."

"Faithful friends are beyond price, no amount can balance their worth."

"Faithful friends are life-saving medicine; those who fear God will find them."

Jesus himself established the church. He sent His disciples out in pairs. He knew the importance of not being isolated. Now Jesus chooses to manifest Himself to us through others and to others through us.

You might ask, "Why do we need community?" One answer can be found in the writings of St. Catherine of Siena. She wrote that God told her, "For I could well have supplied you with all your needs, both spiritual and material. But I wanted to make you dependent on one another."[11]

I once read an interesting comparison. The need for Christian friendship was compared to the necessity of knowing if the brake lights are working on your vehicle. In the days before smart cars with computers, we often only knew if our brake lights were out on our car when someone else pointed this out to us. In much the same way, we as Christians need others to help us know when our spiritual brake lights are not working. Do you need someone to tell you when your spiritual lights are out? I know I did.

In the story of the paralytic found in Luke 5:17-20, we read this:

One day as Jesus was teaching, Pharisees and teachers of the law were sitting there who had come from every village of Galilee and Judea and Jerusalem, and the power of the Lord was with him for healing. And some men brought on a stretcher a man who was paralyzed; they were trying to bring him in and set him in his presence. But not finding a way to bring him in because of the crowd, they went up on the roof and lowered him on the stretcher through the tiles into the middle in front of Jesus. When he saw their faith, he said, "As for you, your sins are forgiven."

These verses cause me to consider that maybe there are times in our lives that our friends, recognizing our broken and wounded condition, need to carry us just like the friends of the paralytic carried him to the saving hands of Jesus. Likewise, if we know our friends are dealing with pain and conflict, and brokenness, we are called to carry them to our Lord. How will our friends know to do this, or how will we know to do this for our friends if either of us is wearing a mask to hide our pain?

LIVING IN COMMUNITY

The lives of the earliest Christians were grounded in communal living. They came together to learn and follow the teaching of the twelve apostles. They formed themselves around daily eucharistic liturgy (i.e., the breaking and sharing of bread). They prayed together. The Bible tells us that as a result of their commitment, the Lord added to their numbers, and many were saved.

Communal Life
They devoted themselves to the teaching of the apostles and to the communal life, to the breaking of the bread and to the prayers. Awe came upon everyone, and many wonders and signs were done through the apostles. All who believed were together and had all things in common; they would sell their property and possessions and divide them among all according to each one's need. Every day they devoted themselves to meeting together in the temple area and to breaking bread in their homes. They ate their meals with exultation and sincerity of heart, praising God and enjoying favor with all the people. And every day **the Lord added to their number those who were being saved.** *-* Acts 2:42-47

If communal living was essential for the early Christians, why should it be any different for us today? Community is still a vital and essential part of being Christian. The gathering of Christians into small groups that meet weekly affords them the opportunity to take their masks off, to be vulnerable, to live openly and honestly, and to share the joys and sorrows of the Christian journey with other caring Christians. The fundamental purpose of these groups is to build deep and meaningful friendships rooted in a common and shared love for Jesus Christ.

Most Christians are active in some type of ministry. The wide variety of ministries each have their own specific reasons to come together. Maybe you sing in the choir, and therefore you come together for choir practice. Maybe you gather weekly with other Christians to work at a soup kitchen to feed the poor. Maybe you are a part of an active Bible study group. All these groups are good, but they are not the type of group gathering that I am talking about here.

Allow me to use the analogy of a modern-day smartphone. Smartphones are capable of many things. They are said to have more computing power than the Apollo rockets. But as powerful as they are, if they are not plugged in to charge their battery, these very smartphones rapidly become worthless pieces of plastic and glass. They must remain charged to carry out the many tasks they are capable of.

The same is true for each of us on our Christian journey. We need to be part of a core group for the purpose of keeping us charged up and functioning properly as we strive to carry out the various tasks we are called to do in the Kingdom of God. A properly functioning group should give energy and sustenance to its members so that they can each live out their individual lives as better Christians.

Are you currently in a group like this? If you are, I applaud you, and what I am about to share may help add a few things to make your group better. If you are not currently in a small Christian group that meets weekly for the purpose I stated above, I want to strongly encourage you to find or start a group for that purpose. Your weekly church bulletin might identify some good groups to join,

While it is important to find friends you can begin to share your journey with, don't overcomplicate this task. Regularly meeting with multiple friends in a group setting is important. But also, if you only have one friend you can trust to regularly meet with, by all means, start meeting. The key is to start. Focus on the need to meet, not the size of the group. Find a friend and find a reason to start sharing. Going forth in this book, I will be referring to these groups as *Christ-Centered Friendship Groups.*

First, I will provide you with a list of some important tips for creating and sustaining a powerful and impactful Christian group. Then I will provide you with a guide for conducting your group discussions.

Each week your group should come together in the same location, if possible. You should follow a prescribed pattern each week. Everyone needs to be given time to share. The gathering should begin and end in prayer.

Keys to a Successful Group

Meet every week at the same time.

Use the Christ-Centered Friendship format listed below as your weekly guide

Try to stay focused on the discussion topics.

Allow a few minutes for each person to share their experience during the past week regarding the topic **BLESSED** first. Next, allow each person to address their **BROKEN** experiences for the week. Finally, allow each person to address the topic of **SHARED**.

Be respectful of your allotted time. Generally, each person only has three to five minutes to share on each topic if you want to keep the meeting to one hour.

Limit your reply to what others say. This is not a time for discussion. It is an opportunity for each person to **share their week's experiences**.

Keep the group time limited to one to one-and-a-half hours.

The ideal group size is three to six people. But like I said earlier, sharing with close friends in whatever group size that's right for you is what's important.

Be open to new members.

Break the group into smaller groups if it grows too large.

Help others to start new groups.

Attend your group even on those days when you don't want to go or feel you have nothing to share.

What is shared in a group stays in a group. **Confidentiality is of utmost importance.**

Never lose sight of the objective. The goal is to build FRIENDSHIPS rooted in our common love for **Jesus Christ**. Don't allow following the mechanics of the meeting to become the goal. Friendship is the goal.

Christ-Centered Friendship Group Meetings
Each week's meeting should begin and end in prayer. The groups I have been involved with begin with a prayer to the Holy Spirit,

while others begin with the Lord's Prayer. Each group can decide what prayer to begin with.

BLESSED

The first topic to discuss is **Blessed.** Here each participant shares how they have been blessed by God in the previous week. The following are suggested discussion topics to keep the meeting on track and prevent the conversation from wandering into discussions about other worldly issues.

> In what way did you most experience God's blessing in your life this week?
>
> How was your prayer life?
>
> What are you studying to learn more about God?
>
> What was the moment that you felt closest to Christ in the past week?
>
> Did God reveal anything new or surprising to you about Himself this week?
>
> Did God reveal anything new or surprising to you about you this week?

BROKEN

The second topic to discuss is **Broken.** During this time, each participant shares either how they have been broken or wounded in the past week. In other words, they openly and transparently share with their friends their struggles. The following is the suggested topic to discuss.

What obstacles and/or sins did you encounter in your life this week that clouded your relationship with God or kept you from being the disciple that you are called to be?

SHARED

The third topic to discuss is **Shared.** At this time in the gathering, each person is given a chance to discuss with their friends how they have shared their faith with others. This is where we reveal our attempts to bring the good news of Christ to others. This is where we report on our evangelical actions.

> After reviewing your blessings and/or brokenness in the previous discussion, what have you learned that you can share with others to help draw them closer to Christ?
>
> How were you an encourager this week to someone who was lost, hurt, or broken?
>
> Did you miss any opportunities to share Christ with someone this week?

Again, I want to emphasize that Jesus is the one who sent the apostles out in pairs. He is the one who established the idea and importance of Christian community. If you want to deepen your relationship with Christ and you want to gain the strength to handle the difficulties of life, I strongly encourage you to join or establish a group and commit to meeting weekly for the balance of your life. I promise you that you will be glad you did.

THREE PERSONALITY TRAITS

Over the past 34 years that I have been participating in these weekly small group gatherings, I have made an interesting observation. Not only does my observation seem to hold true in these small Christian groups, but it seems to hold true in almost every gathering of people.

While I am not a trained psychologist, it appears to me that people can be categorized into three distinct personality groups: Those who draw people in, those who push people away, and those who seem absent-minded to what others in the group are expressing.

I call those in the first group the ENCOURAGERS. They are the ones who draw people in. They are the ones who get people to open up. Simply stated, they encourage others in the group to share their deepest thoughts and feeling.

Encouragers create a safe place for others in the group to be more vulnerable. They make others in the group comfortable about being themselves. Encouragers ask questions like, "Is there something on your mind?" "What's going on in your life?" "How are you feeling today?" "You look like something might be bothering you, is something wrong?" "You are being awfully quiet today, what's bugging you?"

The second group that I have observed I call the INHIBITORS. Those who exhibit this personality trait tend to say things in conversation that push others away. They say things that cause others to be afraid of opening up. They say things that make others keep their innermost thoughts to themselves. What these people say stifles sincere and honest sharing. Inhibitors usually cause others to keep their masks firmly in place. People who are inhibitors rarely know that they are. They have no idea that what they are saying is shutting others down. Permit me to give you a few examples.

After one of my retreats, I had a woman come up to me to share a very painful secret. She told me that she was a member of a small Christian group like I was, encouraging people to join. She went on to tell me that she was afraid to open up to the other ladies in the group about her brokenness. She said that the other ladies in the group frequently made hurtful and disparaging remarks about women whom they heard about or read about that had had abortions.

As it turned out, this woman I was speaking with had had an abortion much earlier in life. It was something she regretted, and it was the area of her deepest brokenness. However, knowing how the others in the group had spoken poorly about women who had abortions, she remained quiet and held in her pain. I was one of the very few people she had ever told. It saddened me to think that she was afraid to open up about her pain to her very best friends. I am sure the other women had no idea how they were hurting one of their friends.

Here is another example of the inhibitor personality trait. Let's assume for a minute that you have developed an addiction to prescription pain medicines. None of your friends know. Today you go to a restaurant with three of your closest Christian friends. You need help, and you know it. Today you intend to open up and share what's going on. In the idle chitchat that takes place as everyone is gathering, someone brings up an article they saw in the newspaper about the large number of people who are addicted to pain medicines. Someone in your group says something like this, "I can't believe that anyone can be so weak-minded that they can become addicted like that." The others chime in with similar disparaging remarks. The conversation signals to you that it is not safe to tell your friends about your struggle. You keep your secret. Your addiction only gets worse.

I want to share just one more example to make my point. Suppose for a moment, much like in the example above, you show up to a meeting of your closest Christian friends. You are deeply embarrassed but want to share with them that you are struggling with an addiction to pornography. This is your best-kept secret. Someone in the group makes a joke about porn addiction based on some recent news report they had just heard. This only serves to make you feel more embarrassed. You leave your group that day with your secret intact. No healing takes place this day. Your struggle continues. The light grows dimmer inside of your wall of shame. Once again, those in the group have no idea how much their banter has hurt you.

I call the third and final personality type the IGNORER. Those who fall into this category neither draw people in like an Encourager nor do they stifle a conversation like an Inhibitor. These people gather with others in the group, and they hear what others are saying, but what they hear simply does not register with them. They don't hear that the other person might be in pain. They might hear someone in the group mention that they are dealing with grief from their father's recent death and somewhat dismiss the importance by saying something like, "Yea, it takes a while to get over grief." What they fail to say is, "How can I be of help to you?" or "Have you considered speaking to a grief counselor about it?" The people with this personality type mean no harm, but they just miss the importance of what someone else is subtly trying to share.

I hope I have clearly articulated the nuances of these three personality types. You might be reading this and trying to determine which one of these personality traits you exhibit. The interesting fact is all of us have all three of these personality types within us. At any time throughout the day, depending on the group dynamic and the discussion topic, we might exhibit any one of these.

Which one do you most want to exhibit? Of course, we all want to be the compassionate and caring Encourager. It is my hope that by bringing this to your attention, you will catch yourself the next time you are being an Inhibitor or an Ignorer and quickly change course. We all need to work hard at becoming the Encourager our Christian faith calls us to be.

If we are going to grow in our faith and relationship with our Lord and if we are going to help others do the same, we must make it a priority to always create a safe zone in our groups for people to freely share their deepest secrets and struggles without fear of any negative reprisal, stigmatization, or gossip. Their sharing needs to be met by your Christ-like concern for their well-being. Sadly, I must tell you that I was in these groups with my closest Christian friends every week for 23 years before I got the courage and felt it was safe enough to reveal my struggles and brokenness.

I feel compelled to make a few key points here. As important as I believe it is to have a safe group of Christian friends with whom we can share honestly and openly about our struggles in life, it is not necessary for us to share these deep wounds with everyone. Remember what it says in Sirach 6:6, *"Let those who are friendly to you be many, but one in a thousand your confidant."* It is essential to have true Christian friends to share with, but some pains are so deep that you would be better advised to share them with a professional counselor or psychologist. Keep in mind, also, that it is critical for our spiritual journey that we share our trials and brokenness with someone. We never want to journey alone, and it is not good for us to hold our brokenness inside. However, telling too many people about our struggles might make them worse. Sirach 6:14 gives us this assurance, *"Faithful friends are a sturdy shelter; whoever finds one finds a treasure."*

Finally, I want to wrap up this chapter on the three personality types with some words of guidance for those times when someone is sharing their struggles with you. This next point is so important that you might want to write it down. When someone shares their pains and struggles with us, what matters most is that we listen. We must also keep in mind that we are not being asked to fix their problem. We are being asked to care. We are called to just be there, to be present, and maybe nothing more. A hug might be more important than words. Romans 12:15 tells us we are called to *"Weep with those who weep."*

Let's take a quick look at three New Testament examples. We first have John. John was the only apostle who did not scatter after Jesus' arrest. He might have been mad and upset at his friends. They had all abandoned Jesus at His most difficult hour. Was there anything John could do to stop the outcome of the crucifixion? No, if he would have tried, the Romans would likely have killed him, too. Even though John could not stop the crucifixion, he stayed with his friend to the end (John 19:26-27). I am sure that seeing him there along the way gave comfort to Jesus in His time of need.

Next, there was Simon of Cyrene. Simon did not stop the crucifixion, but he lightened Jesus' load by helping Him carry the cross (Mt.27:32, Mk 15:21, Lk 23:26). Sometimes we are called to assist in carrying someone else's cross. We are pulled into a difficult situation, and we become part of the shared difficulties of another person. Simon became that person for our Lord.

Finally, as Jesus was hanging on the cross, covered in blood from the nails and from having been scourged, He sees His mother (John 19:25-26). Was there anything Mary could do to stop what was happening? No, there wasn't. Mary was simply present, sharing in the pain of someone she loved. She is present, and she is silent. Her son's grief and pain become her grief and pain—with not a word spoken. However, with that said, I assume that it meant the world to Jesus to see His mother standing nearby.

If you and I care, and if we work at being good Encouragers, we can be there to lighten the load that our friends are carrying, and likewise, they can be there for us.

Ralph Waldo Emerson said it this way, "A day for toil, an hour for sport, but for a friend is life too short."[12]

WOUNDED HEALERS

Up to this point in this section, I have emphasized the importance of how essential it is to be open and honest with others about our weaknesses and struggles. Earlier in the chapter "Broken," I asserted that all of us are broken in some way. When we openly reveal our brokenness to others, it gives them permission to also take their mask off and reveal their struggle in life to us. This is a very healing process, and it is the reason I call this chapter "Wounded Healers."

Think about this, when was Jesus the most effective in His ministry? From my perspective, Jesus was the most effective when He was the most wounded. In Luke 23:34, He says, "Father forgive them." At John 19:30, He said, "It is finished." When Jesus was wounded, tortured, bloodied, and gasping His last breath on the cross, He gave His life in atonement for our sins, thereby granting us the gift of eternal life. Jesus rose victorious on the third day in His glorified body but with His wounds still visible.

What about you and me—are we willing to make our wounds visible if we know that by doing so, we can reveal to others the joy we have experienced through being loved and forgiven by our Savior? When we share with others the redemption that we have experienced through Jesus Christ from the sins that held us captive for so long, we give them hope. They begin to realize that Jesus loves them, too, despite their brokenness.

As I stated at the beginning of this book, St. Augustine tells us that to know God, we must know ourselves. John Denver sang the song, *Tenderly Calling*. The song makes the point that we should not attempt to run away from the storms in our life. If we are going to make forward progress in our conversion, we must be willing to move beyond our fear, stand up, and truthfully look at our own reflection in the mirror. In the silence of our reflection, we just might hear the quiet voice of Jesus calling us home. With Christ at our side, we can make it through any tempest that blows up in our life.

The thought of taking time to deeply reflect on our lives can be scary. The thought of revealing to others the brokenness that we see within can be likened to the raging storm mentioned in the song. To draw closer to our Lord, we must break down the walls of shame that keep us isolated and alone in our darkness. We must stand up and face our reflections. We must come to grips with both the good and the bad that lies within us. Once we are brave enough to openly reveal our faults to others, the tempest inside will calm down. In the vulnerability of our honest sharing, we can experience a deep encounter with Christ through the person we are sharing with. It is at this point that we experience the joy of the prodigal son returning home to the father.

EXERCISE THREE

THE MIRROR EXERCISE

During the retreats that I conduct, each attendee is given a small round mirror. I instruct them to hold the mirror and stare deeply into their own eyes. So, I now ask you to go look into a mirror. If you don't have access to a mirror, you can always use your cell phone's camera in selfie mode.

Stare deeply into your own eyes as I ask the following questions:

> Do you see the real you?
>
> Do you see a sinner?
>
> Do you see someone who has either been wounded by the world or broken by sin?
>
> Do you see some well-guarded secrets?
>
> Do you see someone chained by some area of sinfulness?
>
> Does anyone else really know the REAL you?

Now, as you reflect on the person looking back at you in the mirror, think about this: God loves you so much that He gave His only Son so that you could believe in Him and have eternal life.

God knew you in the womb before you were even born. God knew every sin you would ever commit. He loves the person you are looking at in the mirror so much that if you were the only person alive, He still would have sent His Son to save you. If God loves you this much, can you begin to love the person in the mirror as much as God does? Can you forgive the person in the mirror like God already has? We need to work hard at seeing the person that God sees, and we need to love that person that God loves.

Permit me to share a story that illustrates this point. Suppose for a minute that you are driving eastbound in your car during the early morning hours. The sun is glaring brightly through your windshield. How does your windshield look? I suspect that you can see every smudge mark, every dirt spot, every smashed bug, and all the crystallization of the glass that has occurred from dirt and debris hitting it. In summary, when the sun is glaring through your windshield, it looks like a mess.

Now drive that same car at night. Assume there are no cars coming from the other direction. You are driving into the darkness. How does that windshield look? It looks clear. When there is no light shining through the windshield from the outside, there is nothing to illuminate the imperfections on the glass.

The same is true in our own lives. When we stare into the mirror, it is the SON OF GOD, not the sun, who illuminates our flaws. He does this in a loving and gentle way so that we can be aware of our imperfections and work at making necessary changes in our life. If, on the other hand, we looked into the mirror and everything looked just fine, if we saw no imperfections, it might be an indication that we are heading towards the darkness. We need to understand that seeing and being aware of our shortcomings and sins is not a bad thing. In fact, seeing these imperfections is a gift from

God. He loves us so much that He desires to reveal these to us so that we can repent and experience His amazing forgiveness, love, and mercy.

As we learn to love and befriend the wounded and broken person that we were staring at in the mirror, we become better at loving the broken people we meet and encounter every day with Christ-like love. This is what I mean when I say we are called to be WOUNDED HEALERS.

Pope Francis said it this way, **"The more conscious we are of our wretchedness and our sins, the more we experience the love and infinite mercy of God among us, then the more capable we are of looking upon the many 'wounded' we meet along the way with acceptance and mercy."**[13]

Think about this. Jesus was His most effective in His public ministry when He was the most wounded. When He was hanging on the cross, and when He gasped His last breath, He healed humanity. He gave His life so that all who would believe in Him would be saved. Jesus was the ultimate wounded healer. As followers of Jesus, we must do as He did. Even though we are wounded, we need to go out to share with others the good news that Jesus loves us even though we are far from perfect. We need to let them know that Jesus loves them, too, no matter how broken they might be. When we do this, we are being Eucharist for others. We are, at that moment, Blessed, Broken, and Shared.

MOONGLOW

Now I would like to make a very important point. I am going to use the moon as an analogy to make this point. Mankind has been writing about, singing songs about, and reciting poems about the moon for as long as we have been on the planet. It has left its imprint on our language, art, mythology, and, of course, the lunar calendar. We love to romanticize the moon.

What is it about the moon that has captured the heart of man? To answer that question, we must first understand both what the moon is and what it isn't. To start with, contrary to children's fairy tales, the moon is not made of cheese. It is widely believed that the moon was formed from debris left from an impact between Earth and another large planet-sized space object. Phrases like dead surface or dry lava lakes are often used to describe the surface of the moon. Essentially, the moon is a space rock. You might even say that since it is leftover debris, the moon is truly space junk.

So, you might ask if it is space junk, why is it so romanticized? It is the light of the moon that has captured our attention. After the sun, the moon is the second-brightest celestial object regularly visible in Earth's sky. However, the moon itself emits no light. The moon's surface is dark. The moon merely reflects the light of the sun. It is the light of the sun, reflecting off this large piece of space junk that we find so beautiful.

What is the purpose of me using this analogy? Due to our wounded and broken condition as human beings, one could say that we are like the moon. Like the moon's surface, we are covered with the scars of our past sins. Metaphorically speaking, we can be likened to space junk. If we, as "space junk," are going to bring light to those around us, we must realize that our light comes from Jesus Christ.

Now, this is where my metaphor breaks down. Unlike the moon, which reflects the light of the SUN, we are *not* called to reflect the light of the SON of God. You see, the moon has no light within it. It can only reflect light. You and I can *radiate* a light from within.

The Bible makes it clear that the light of Christ and His Holy Spirit reside inside of us. I invite you to read these verses.

Romans 8:10: *But if Christ is in you, although the body is dead because of sin, the spirit is alive because of righteousness.*

Galatians 2:20: *Yet I live, no longer I, but Christ lives in me; insofar as I now live in the flesh, I live by faith in the Son of God who has loved me and given himself up for me.*

I Corinthians 6:19: *Do you not know that your body is a temple of the holy Spirit within you, whom you have from God, and that you are not your own?*

Despite our broken condition, we have the assurance that God dwells within us. Therefore, we are called not to merely reflect the light of Christ, but rather we are called to RADIATE HIS LIGHT to everyone around us.

A BROKEN DOOR

Earlier in the book, I told the story of the Parable of The Broken Door. I became so captivated by the analogy of a broken door that I named my ministry Broken Door Ministries. Let's take a moment to take one more look at this broken door concept.

I want to stress the point that it is possible to enter a home even if the door is broken and barely hanging from the hinges. Likewise, we need to spend our lives allowing others to enter into our lives to encounter Christ inside of us, yes, even though we ourselves are broken.

Far too often, Christians, out of scrupulosity, take the position that they are unworthy to evangelize because they are not perfect. If being perfect was the key element to answering the call of God, Moses, King David, St. Paul, and countless other saints over the years would have been excluded. Our baptism makes us worthy. We know from St. Paul in 1Cor1:26 that God delights in calling those who are seemingly unqualified. In 1Tim.1:12, we read that God judges us worthy when He calls us. By virtue of our baptism, we are called to bring others into the family of God, to be evangelizers.

It is precisely because of our brokenness that we become ideal evangelizers. We have a personal story to tell. We have been given the opportunity to share the good news of the love and mercy

Jesus bestowed on us with others. This gives them the hope that they, too, can be saved.

After healing the deaf man who had a speech impediment, Mark 7:36 tells us that Jesus ordered the man not to tell anyone. Reading further, however, we see that the more He ordered those He had healed not to tell what had occurred, the more they proclaimed it. It is hard to contain the excitement of having a personal healing encounter with Jesus. We, like the deaf man, should enthusiastically proclaim our joy to everyone who will listen to our story.

We must never forget that a broken door can still allow entry to someone who, once inside, might encounter the perfect door of Jesus Christ. I end each of my weekly podcasts by saying this, "Be the door, no matter how broken you might be, through which others can enter to encounter Christ." This is also why I have handed out wristbands to those who attend my retreats that say, **"BE THE DOOR."**

ENCOUNTERING CHRIST IN OUR VULNERABILITY

Let me be crystal clear about something, vulnerability is scary. I have written a lot about the importance of making our brokenness known to others. This is certainly a painful process. Jesus implores us to get beyond our pride, humble ourselves, and become vulnerable. It's as if He is cheering us on, urging us along the way. Still, this isn't easy, and it isn't fun. I was terrified to do it for 42 years of my life.

But allow me to take us back to the beginning of the book. There I said that Jesus took the bread. In other words, He chose a specific piece of bread. Likewise, God specifically chooses you. He calls us with full knowledge of our broken condition to be evangelizers.

Of course, as I stated in the beginning, to make our brokenness known, we must know ourselves well. This requires us to go on a scary trip. I call this the "Journey Through Hell." We must embark on a daunting journey into the deepest and darkest areas of our soul.

Let's face it, we all have evil inside of us. Our pride and ego attempt to block our ability to see the evil inside us and see ourselves as we really are. They work in concert to blind us to our flaws and sins. In addition to pride and ego, shame steps up to paralyze us.

It nags us with the notion that we are a bad person. We fear having our flaws exposed to others.

But truly, we are no different than most people. Mark 7:20-23 tells us, *"From within people, from their hearts, come evil thoughts, unchastity, theft, murder, adultery, greed, malice, deceit, licentiousness, envy, blasphemy, arrogance, folly. All these evils come from within and they defile."*

Most of us work hard to make a good impression on others. We are all shined up on the outside. But inside, we find the rust and corrosion of sin. In Matthew 23:28, Jesus describes us, *"On the outside you appear righteous, but inside you are filled with hypocrisy and evildoing."* In verse 26, He says, *"Blind Pharisee, cleanse first the inside of the cup, so that the outside also may be clean."*

As I write this, we are living in a time where sanitizing has become increasingly important. Because of the Coronavirus pandemic, we are told endlessly to wash our hands and use hand sanitizer. I wonder if we are as fastidious about cleaning our soul from evil as we are about ridding ourselves of Covid-19.

We cannot allow shame to keep us from becoming vulnerable and honest with ourselves and with others about the things in our life that separate us from God. We are not alone in our sinfulness. Romans 3:23 tells us, *"All have sinned and are deprived of the glory of God."* In 1 John 1:8-9, we read, *"If we say, 'We are without sin,' we deceive ourselves, and the truth is not in us. If we acknowledge our sins, he is faithful and just and will forgive our sins and cleanse us from every wrongdoing."*

My friends, recurring sins dull our conscience. Left unchecked, they can lead to our separation from God. We must be willing to confront our inner evil. Sin is real, and the need for repentance is real. Every sin we commit inflicts yet another wound on the Body of Christ, the very One who came to save us from our sin.

In addition to wreaking havoc on us personally, sin wreaks havoc upon others around us. We think that sin harms only us. But in truth, as a community of believers, as we read in 1Cor 12:26, "If one member suffers, all suffer together." Our sin caused others to suffer, too.

To break free from this suffering and the chains that bind us and to draw closer to God, we must be willing to journey through the hell inside. Taking stock of our evil side helps us to repent more honestly. If we fail to journey into our inner hell, we run the risk of becoming complacent about our sins. If we fail to acknowledge our sins, they will clearly enslave us.

When we muster the courage to tell others about our wounds and brokenness, we break the chains of shame that bind us, and the darkness that exists inside of us will become filled with Jesus Christ and become as bright as the noonday sun.

As we become more aware of ourselves and our flaws, we also come face to face with God and His mercy. It is in this encounter with God that we receive the courage to tell others about what God has done for us.

Opening up with others requires our humility. We are humbled when we accept the reality that we are flawed and sinful persons. Humility is a good thing. In 1 Peter 5:6-7, we read, *"So humble yourselves under the mighty hand of God, that he may exalt you in due time. Cast all your worries upon him because he cares for you."*

We know that God has a long history of using broken people to bring about good things in His Kingdom. St. Paul confirms this in his words from 1 Corinthians 1:26-31, *"God chose the foolish of the world to shame the wise, and God chose the weak of the world to shame the strong, and God chose the lowly and despised of the world, those who count for nothing, to reduce to nothing those who are something, so that no human being might boast before God."*

Dear friends, I am not encouraging you to tell others about the broken aspects of your life to bring undue attention to your sins. No, I am asking you to be open and become vulnerable about your sins to bring honor and glory to the One, Jesus Christ, who saves you from those sins. St. Paul says it this way, *"I will rather boast most gladly of my weaknesses, in order that the power of Christ may dwell with me"* (1 Corinthians 12:9).

As we confront our demons, we more clearly see that we must die to ourselves so that Christ can live in us. We will know God to the extent we are set free from ourselves.

So, let me ask you some very important questions. Are you going to remain s*cared* by your wounds and flaws, or will you, for the sake of Jesus Christ, shed your pride, kick down the walls of shame, become vulnerable, and *share* your brokenness and wounded self and your utter dependence on Jesus Christ with others?

I can assure you of this—the sharing of my brokenness has turned out to be a great blessing in my life. Through my open and honest sharing, I have found release, a freedom I can't really explain, except it comes from God's grace and from a closer walk with Christ. My fervent prayer is that by sharing your brokenness, you, too, will break free, find freedom, and find the courage to shout from the mountain tops your love for our Savior.

TWO HEROES

Every good book needs a hero, and this book has two of them. Both heroes in this book were extremely important in my spiritual journey. Let me set the stage for their introduction.

Several times in this book, I have mentioned the life-changing silent retreat that I made in 2011. In the "Scared" chapter, I told you that I felt God speaking directly to my heart on the third night of the retreat with these words, *"Brian, if you want to heal, you have to tell someone you are broken."* As that chapter continued, I revealed my brokenness to you. I told you what was written on both sides of my Purple Paper. My story has been told in this book, and I describe it every time I put on a Blessed, Broken, and Scared retreat. It gets a little easier to tell the story each time. But what I want to share with you now is how difficult it was the first time I followed God's instructions and told someone about my brokenness.

Immediately after returning home from making my silent retreat, many of my closest Christian friends asked me about my experience. They wanted to know what I had discovered on that retreat. Several people were curious about my main takeaway from the retreat. Each time I was asked, I answered by telling them exactly what God told me. I repeated the words, *"Brian, if you want to heal, you have to tell someone you are broken."* For nearly a year, I told my story over and over again. But there was a problem. I was only telling half the story. I was leaving out the embarrassing part of the story. Yes, I told those who asked that I had been molested and that I had held that inside for 42 years. What I failed to share was the part about how that event left me broken. I was still holding back. I was only revealing side one of my Purple Paper.

As you recall from my previous discussion about the Purple Paper, I ask everyone on a retreat to write something on both sides of the paper. On side one, they write down how they have been wounded by the world. On side two, I have them write down their primary recurring sin. St. Paul tells us in Romans 6:6 that we become *"slaves to sin."* I ask people to write down the one sin that continually enslaves them.

For ten months after my retreat, I spoke to the men in my weekly friendship group reunion, as it's known to people who have made a Cursillo weekend, about the revelation God put on my heart. "To be healed," I would tell them, "we must tell someone we are broken." This always led to lively discussions, but never once did it lead anyone to open up and share their struggles, me included. But that was about to change.

THE FIRST HERO

On Thursday, August 2, 2012, I joined up with two friends of mine, both named Bob. Together we drove another man from Hendersonville, North Carolina, to Charlotte so that he could make his Cursillo weekend. We dropped him off at St. Ann Catholic Church in Charlotte and began our two-hour, 105-mile trip back to Hendersonville. On the trip home, the conversation once again turned to the topic of brokenness. I asked both Bobs the following two questions, "Guys, do you ever have something deep and troubling inside that you want to share, but it seems to get stuck in your throat? Do you ever get the story of what you want to share as far as your lips, but then you can't seem to say it?" Both men, in near perfect unison, said, "Yep…. yep… I sure do."

After saying that, the conversation in the car fell silent. So here we were, three really good friends, riding in the car, all admitting that we hold things inside that we wish we had the courage to share, but not one of us shared a thing. An eerie silence floated in the air like a heavy fog for the remainder of the ride home. Before long, our trip concluded. They dropped me off at my home, with my brokenness still safely hidden. The conversation had ended, at least that is what I thought.

A few days after our trip, I received an email from one of the two Bobs. The email said something like this, "Brian, it seemed as if you had something weighing heavy on your heart that you wanted to share in the car the other evening. If you want to talk, I am here for you." Sadly, I deleted that email.

Bob, however, persisted. A few days later, I received a second email from Bob. This one said something like this, "Brian, I am not sure if you read the email that I sent you a few days ago, but it seemed as if you had something weighing heavy on your heart that you wanted to share in the car the other evening. If you want to talk, I am here for you." I guess I still was not sure I had the courage to discuss this, so once again, I deleted his email.

It may have been a week later when a third email from Bob appeared in my inbox. The message was essentially the same as the first two. As I read the email, my mind immediately recalled the story of Peter denying Christ three times.

This is the story from Luke 22:54-62: *After arresting him they led him away and took him into the house of the high priest; Peter was following at a distance. They lit a fire in the middle of the courtyard and sat around it, and Peter sat down with them. When a maid saw him seated in the light, she looked intently at him and said, "This man too was with him." But he denied it saying, "Woman, I do not know him." A short while later someone else saw him and said, "You too are one of them"; but Peter answered, "My friend, I am not." About an hour later, still another insisted, "Assuredly, this man too was with him, for he also is a Galilean." But Peter said, "My friend, I do not know what you are talking about." Just as he was saying this, the cock crowed, and the Lord turned and looked at Peter; and Peter remembered the word of the Lord, how he had said to him, "Before the cock crows today, you will deny me three times." He went out and began to weep bitterly.*

I realized at that moment that Bob was trying to be Christ to me. He was reaching out to help me. I had already denied him twice. I did not want to deny him a third time. This time I replied to his email with these words, "Where and when would you like to meet?" We set a time to meet on September 27, 2012. Of all places to have this important discussion, we chose to meet at a frozen yogurt store. There, for the first time in my life, over a cup of frozen yogurt, I opened up to someone other than my wife about the struggles I had been dealing with for over 40 years.

What happened next is what blew me away. My friend asked me to stand up. He then said something like this, "Brian, I have always admired you and thought highly of you. It must have been very hard to share that with me. I admire you even more because of your courage." With that said, he gave me a big hug. Even though it was Bob giving me the hug, I felt the warm embrace of Jesus Christ at that moment. It was a life-altering encounter. And at that moment, Bob became one of the heroes of this story.

I want to make a vitally important point here. At the exact moment that I spoke to Bob and told him about my life-long struggles, I felt a profound peace come over me. The peace was short-lived, however. At the conclusion of our meeting, as soon as I got back into my car to drive home, Satan instantly jumped on my shoulders and began whispering negative thoughts in my ears. He said things like: *"You are a fool for telling someone about your personal struggles,"* and *"Telling someone about such personal struggles will certainly come back to haunt you.* I instantly began to doubt my decision. I used the phrase, *"Get behind me Satan"* in the hope that he would stop. With prayer and with time, that peace eventually returned.

I knew in my heart that I did what God told me to do. Therefore I trusted in God and held tight to the belief that I did the right thing. Time has proven so. This is a critically important point because opening up about our struggles is never easy. It is scary, and

Satan always uses fear to try to make us doubt God's love, mercy, and forgiveness. I would be less than honest if I did not tell you that even to this day, Satan still tries to use doubt every once in a while to distract me from my mission to share the story of God's mercy and love. His attack is relentless. I hold firmly to my trust in Jesus. We always have the words of our Savior, *"Be not afraid,"* to hold on to.

I will likely never know if I would have found the courage to do what God told me to do on that retreat if my friend Bob did not persist in pulling it out of me. He did not give up after just one email and one attempt. He sensed that I was hurting, and he continued to try to help. I received a healing miracle in my life because my good friend Bob demonstrated exactly what it means to be an ENCOURAGER. Without Bob's actions, I might never have gained the courage to discuss my brokenness, and this book, and my ministry, would never have happened.

The first time you tell another person about your brokenness is the hardest time. Each subsequent time you bring it up, it gets a little easier. The most astonishing thing in all of this is discovering that rather than people pulling away from you because you revealed your brokenness, the exact opposite seems to occur. People are drawn to your courage, candor, and sincerity. Because I have been willing to open up about my struggles in life, thousands of people over the past several years have opened up to me about theirs. Their healing process was put into motion because they found a safe place and a safe person to share with.

Yes, Bob truly is a hero in my life and in this book! Thank you, Bob!

THE SECOND HERO

As I said, there are two heroes. The second hero is my wife. Not only was my wife the very first and, for a long time, the only person I had told about having been molested, but she has journeyed with me for 44 of the 63 years of my life. She has seen the best and the worst of me. She has been there in the good times and in the bad times.

Since starting this ministry, she has become the sounding board for my weekly writings, and she has become my traveling companion on our ministry road trips.

In 2014 I suddenly became blind, and I was subsequently diagnosed with a very rare neurological illness called MOG. I have regained some of my sight, but I now have permanently damaged vision, and I am slowly losing the ability to walk. She has been at my side throughout this illness, and since it is no longer safe for me to drive due to this disability, she is the person that drives us to all of our retreats. During the retreats, she helps me set up and take down everything needed for a successful retreat experience. She also runs the soundboard.

This means that she is subjected to listening to me tell the same stories to different audiences around the country, over and over again. She listens as I speak of my brokenness. And as painful as it is, not only does she listen as I tell the story of having been sexually molested, but she also hears me speak of my struggles with lust and unchaste behavior.

But here is the real point I want to make. What truly makes her the hero of this story is the example she gives us all about how to respond to someone with mercy and love.

As I have told you, God made it clear to me on my retreat that I needed to open up about the broken areas of my life. Following that retreat, my wife was the first person that I needed to become more transparent and open with. She had known since before we were married that I had been sexually molested. She was the only person who ever knew. What she didn't know, however, is how much it had impacted my life on the inside. Now it was time to tell her. As soon as I got in my car to make the 10-hour drive home from Clearwater to the Carolinas, I knew I had to call her. As I started up the car, I prayed for courage. Then I broke my eight days of silence with a cell phone call to my wife. As I drove, we talked for hours.

Over the next several months, she and I had many long, detailed conversations about the areas of struggle in my life. I opened up to her about my struggles with lust. I explained how having been molested left me with some distorted views of healthy sexuality. The more I shared, the more she cared! The more I opened up and let her into the wounded areas of my life, the deeper our love for each other grew. The more transparent I became, the closer we became.

Finally, one day as we were driving together in the car, during a long discussion, she said the words I will never forget, **"Brian, if part of you is broken, then I love that part, too, because I love all of you."** Her caring comment left me speechless. I cried. At that precise time, my wife was being Christ to me. She demonstrated what unconditional love is truly all about.

During my retreats, I put these words up on the screen for all to see. I leave them on the screen in a moment of silence so that they can sink into the minds and hearts of everyone in attendance. Then I advance to the next slide. This next slide leaves a lasting impact on the people attending the retreat. I explain that the words on the next slide are a message from God to everyone in the room. Here is what it says on the next slide, *"If part of you is broken, then I love that part, too, because I love all of you,"* signed **GOD**! This is also the message that I want everyone reading this book to take to heart.

As I stated above, not only is my wife my hero, but in that instance, she was being Christ to me. She demonstrated the meaning of unconditional love. Her loving response gave me the courage in time to reveal my brokenness to others. I have become an open book to my friends and family and to those who attend my retreats, and now to those who are reading this book.

She and my friend Bob have both given us all a lesson on how we should respond to others. I will be forever grateful for their loving response.

INWARD-UPWARD-OUTWARD

As Christians, we should be mission-focused people—you and I have been called to help build the Kingdom of God. The great commissioning from Matthew 28:19-20 states, *"Go, therefore, and make disciples of all nations, baptizing them in the name of the Father, and of the Son, and of the holy Spirit, teaching them to observe all that I have commanded you. And behold, I am with you always, until the end of the age."*

Assuming we are willing to undertake this Christian outreach, we must be quick to remember the words of my pastor, "You must also understand that you, too, have your own areas of sin and brokenness that impact your life. Until you come to grips with your own brokenness, you will never be as effective evangelizing others as God intends for you to be." In other words, my pastor was giving me a starting place.

We all know that every journey in life begins with that first step. One of the most important first steps for us as Christians is to take a hard, honest look at ourselves. This is not our destination; it is our starting point on a long journey. But we must take this step. There is an old expression that states, "The only way to eat an elephant is one bite at a time."

When we take this first step, spiritually speaking, we must be willing to be honest, humble, and stand naked before God. After all, nothing is hidden from God. In Hebrews 4:12, we read, *"And there is no creature hidden from His sight, but all things are naked and open to the eyes of Him to whom we must give account."* In Luke 12:2-3, we also read, *"There is nothing concealed that will not be revealed, nor secret that will not be known. Therefore, whatever you have said in the darkness will be heard in the light."*

On November 21, 2018, during his weekly general audience in St. Peter's Square, Pope Francis said, "Blessed are those who recognize their evil desires and, with a penitent and humiliated heart, stand before God and humanity, not as one of the righteous, but as a sinner." To be effective evangelizers, we must do this. The Apostle Paul said this in 1 Timothy 1:15, *"Christ Jesus came into the world to save sinners. Of these I am the foremost."* Peter said this to Jesus in Luke 5:8 *"Depart from me, Lord, for I am a sinful man."*[14]

We all have our dark side. We have all sinned. Too often, we try to hide our sins from others, from ourselves, and we even try to hide them from God. We must stop doing this. Ephesians 5:6-20 tells us, *"For you were once darkness, but now you are light in the Lord. Live as children of light."* It continues by telling us, *"Everything exposed by the light becomes visible, for everything that becomes visible is light."* Jesus is the light that illuminates our sins, so we can acknowledge them and receive His forgiveness.

Numbers 21:4-9 gives us the story about the Israelites speaking against God and against Moses. When they did, God sent poisonous serpents among them. The serpents bit the people, and they died. The Lord said to Moses, *"Make a poisonous serpent, and set it on a pole; and everyone who is bitten shall look at it and live."* God used the serpent as a symbol of their sinfulness. When they looked honestly at their own sinful actions, they found healing.

We see this story repeated in John 3:14-21 when Jesus tells Nicodemus, *"And just as Moses lifted up the serpent in the desert, so must the Son of Man be lifted up, so that everyone who believes in him may have eternal life."* When you and I look at the crucified Christ, we see our sins. We see our loving Lord, who took our sins and allowed them to be nailed to the cross.

The first step then is to look INWARD, but we can't stop here. If we do, we engage in little more than a useless navel-gazing exercise. If we stop here, we will fall victim to analysis paralysis. Clearly, the cross forces us to acknowledge our failures and shortcomings. But in the crucified Christ, we see something much more. We see the one who bore our sins on the cross. When we gaze at our Lord on the cross, we see our salvation. John 3:16 tells us, *"For God so loved the world that he gave his only Son, so that everyone who believes in him might not perish but might have eternal life."*

This leads to the important second step, which is to look UPWARD. We must look up at the cross in order to give thanks to God for the gift of His Son Jesus the Christ. We thank Him for the gift of grace and salvation in our own life, and we ask God to strengthen us as we accept His challenges to take the message of His love, forgiveness, and mercy out to others. Having acknowledged our own brokenness and having recognized the amazing gift of God's mercy, given to us through the death and resurrection of His Son Jesus, we now have a story to tell others.

We are now finally prepared to go OUTWARD. Yes, we now have our own story to share, and God has called us to share it in order to draw others unto Himself. This may seem daunting. Where and how do we begin? There is an old Cursillo expression that tells us to begin right where we are. It goes like this, "Bloom where you are planted."

None of us is an island unto ourselves. We all live out our life in various environments. Some environments are common to almost everyone, like our family, church, work, and neighborhood environments. In addition, most of us have other unique environments as well. Perhaps you are a member of a sports team or an alumni group or member of a book club, or some other social environment. It is in all of these environments that we can begin the process of sharing the *"Good News"* of what Jesus has done for us. It is with the people in these environments that we can sing, "I once was lost, but now I'm found, was blind, but now I see."

The inward-upward-outward journey could be summed up by a quote that is often attributed to St. Francis, "Start by doing what is necessary, then what is possible, and suddenly you are doing the impossible."

Without first acknowledging our brokenness and our need for a Savior, we really have no story to share. But once we look with honesty in the mirror at our flaws and sinfulness and once we accept Jesus as our Savior and experience His awesome gifts of love, mercy, and forgiveness, we now have a story to share that can change the world. The formula is simple. We must look inward, upward, and we must go outward. Go out to your various environments and tell your story. This is evangelization. This is the mission. This is one of the ways we build God's kingdom. This is the journey of a Christian.

CALLED

THE CALL

> *"Rejoice always. Pray without ceasing. In all circumstances give thanks, for this is the will of God for you in Christ Jesus."*
> 1 Thessalonians 5:16-18

By this point, you may be experiencing the whisper of the Holy Spirit. If you are now willing to acknowledge your own brokenness and you are praying for the courage to tell someone about it, what must happen next? God does not shine light on our sinfulness and brokenness to bring attention to our sins and pains, but He draws attention to these things so that He can demonstrate the healing power and the mercy of His Son Jesus Christ. These personal encounters give us a story to tell. What will we do with our story? Will we bury our story, like the servant who buried His master's money? Or will we be like the leper that we read about in Mark 1:45 who was cleansed, and even though Jesus instructed him to tell no one, he went away and began to publicize the whole matter?

Once we have a truly healing encounter with the mercy of God, it is hard to contain the joy. The Bible has many examples of people who, once they had an encounter with Jesus, felt the call to go forth. Will we go forth? Let's take a look at a few examples.

Mathew 4:18-22: *"As he was walking by the Sea of Galilee, he saw two brothers, Simon who is called Peter, and his brother Andrew, casting a net into the sea; they were fishermen. He said to them,* **"Come after me**, *and I will make you fishers of men."* **At once** *they left their nets and followed him. He walked along from there and saw two other brothers, James, the son of Zebedee, and his brother John. They were in a boat, with their father Zebedee, mending their nets. He called them, and* **immediately** *they left their boat and their father and followed him."*

Mathew 9:9-13: *As Jesus passed on from there, he saw a man named Matthew sitting at the customs post. He said to him,* **"Follow me." And he got up and followed him.** *While he was at table in his house, many tax collectors and sinners came and sat with Jesus and his disciples. The Pharisees saw this and said to his disciples, "Why does your teacher eat with tax collectors and sinners?" He heard this and said, "Those who are well do not need a physician, but the sick do. Go and learn the meaning of the words, "I desire mercy, not sacrifice.* **I did not come to call the righteous but sinners."**

John 4:25-28: *The woman said to him, "I know that the Messiah is coming, the one called the Anointed; when he comes, he will tell us everything." Jesus said to her, "I am he, the one who is speaking with you." At that moment his disciples returned, and were amazed that he was talking with a woman, but still no one said, "What are you looking for?" or "Why are you talking with her?" The woman left her water jar and went into the town and said to the people.*

John 4:39-40: *Many of the Samaritans of that town began to believe in him because of the word of the woman who testified, "He told me everything I have done. When the Samaritans came to him, they invited him to stay with them; and he stayed there two days.*

Mark 1:40-45 *A leper came to him [and kneeling down] begged him and said, "If you wish, you can make me clean." Moved with pity, he* *stretched out his hand, touched him, and said to him, "I do will it. Be made clean." The leprosy left him immediately, and he was made clean. Then, warning him sternly, he dismissed him at once. Then he said to him,* **"See that you tell no one anything***, but go, show yourself to the priest and offer for your cleansing what Moses prescribed; that will be proof for them."* **The man went away and began to publicize the whole matter***. He spread the report abroad so that it was impossible for Jesus to enter a town openly. He remained outside in deserted places, and people kept coming to him from everywhere.*

Mark1:29-31: *On leaving the synagogue he entered the house of Simon and Andrew with James and John. Simon's mother-in-law lay sick with a fever. They immediately told him about her. He approached, grasped her hand, and helped her up.* **Then the fever left her, and she waited on them.**

In my case, I felt compelled to share my story. Just like the others, I did not do it to draw attention to my brokenness and sins. I did so because I could not contain my joy, and I couldn't wait to tell others how Jesus healed me and made me whole.

I think you will be quite surprised in the next chapter when I describe the next step on this healing journey. For now, let us rejoice in the knowledge that God has called us to go forth to share the good news.

A SEA OF PURPLE

If we say, "We are without sin," we deceive ourselves, and the truth is not in us. - *1 John 1:8*

This is one of THE most important chapters in the book. As we approach the end, I want to bring your attention to how the attendees at my retreats feel as we draw close to the end of the retreat. At that point, many people in attendance think they have the primary message of the retreat figured out. They assume that my principal objective is to get them to confront their struggles and shortcomings, take their masks off, become vulnerable and go tell others about their wounds and need for Jesus and how He gave them peace and healing. As important as these things are, there is an even more important principle that cannot be overlooked.

We just learned in the last two chapters that we are called by God to have an outward-focused life. We are challenged to go out to help others and bring them to a closer relationship with Christ. If my primary objective were to encourage you to reveal your brokenness, it would be an inwardly focused objective rather than an outwardly focused objective.

Now, think about this. Everyone attending the retreats has a Purple Paper in their pocket. Yes, everyone! If the pastor is present, he has one. If various ministry leaders are there, they have one. If church council members are there, they have one. Every single person in attendance has a Purple Paper, and written on the two sides of that Purple Paper are their wounds and their most frequently recurring sins. That Purple Paper, which is folded up in their pocket, contains their most well-guarded secrets.

At this point in the retreat, each person is still myopically focused on only their own Purple Paper, and they haven't stopped to realize that every other person in attendance has one, too. At this time, I instruct everyone to look around the room and make eye contact with at least two other people. Then I say these words, "Look around you, you are living in a virtual SEA OF PURPLE."

The same is true for you dear readers. Everyone reading this book, if they are honest, has something written down on their Purple Paper as well. Everyone does! Everyone else is equally as good at hiding behind their mask as you are. Nearly everyone tries to hide their sins and wounds from others.

Okay, I feel like we need a drum roll at this point. I need to draw 100 percent of your attention to what I am about to say. Here it comes. Are you ready? This is so vitally important. You should highlight the next paragraph and/or write it down in your notes.

Even though God spoke directly to my heart during that silent retreat and told me, *"Brian, if you want to be healed, you have to tell someone you are broken,"* I did not run right out and do it. Nearly one year later, I still had not told anyone about my wounds and brokenness. Shame still had its grip on me. Then a miracle took place. My friend Bob cared enough about me to essentially pull this information out of me. I finally made it known only after someone helped me to make it known. Even God's own words weren't enough to get me to open up. God worked through Bob to help me.

Since I did not immediately respond to God's prompting, there is little or no chance that you will do so simply because of my prompting. The good news is this; there is a better solution. I promise you it works. Here is what I am really asking you to do. I want you to commit to spending the rest of your life helping others to reveal the brokenness and wounds that are written down on their Purple Paper. If you do for others what Bob did for me, God in His time will place you in the right circumstance so that someone else will help you reveal your Purple Paper, too. This is what is meant by living an outward-focused life.

I read an article that drives home how important this is. It was an interview with a mother who had recently lost her son to suicide. This mother poured out her emotions. She would have done anything possible to save her son. Then she said these words, and they are indelibly planted in my brain. Here is what she said, **"It's hard to heal wounds you cannot see!"**

You and I are called to bring the good news of Jesus to hurting and wounded people. Others are called to do the same thing for us. But, as long as we all hide behind our masks, that mother's words from the interview will ring true. It will be impossible to heal wounds none of us can see.

The next time you are at church, try asking someone this question, "How are you today?" Nearly 100 percent of the time, you will get the same answer. They will respond by saying, "I'm fine." I can tell you from experience that "I'm fine" is almost never a true statement. When they say it, follow up with this question in your most caring voice, "No, how are you? I really care." Be prepared because the real answer will start to come out. You will not hear "I'm fine" to your second question.

People will respond with a myriad of things like, "Well, my

spouse is sick," or they might say, "My child recently had some problems," or possibly, "We just put my mother-in-law in a nursing home." They might even tell you something like, "I just entered into an alcohol recovery program," or "I just lost my job," or "I was just diagnosed with cancer." The one answer you will not get when you truly let them know that you care is, "I'm fine."

Everywhere we go and everyone we encounter every day has a Purple Paper even if they don't know or acknowledge it. Our family members, our work colleagues, the grocery store clerk, and even the people sitting around us in church every Sunday have a Purple Paper. We live in a *Sea of Purple*.

When you internalize this important reality, you will change the way you interact with others. You will see the importance of becoming an Encourager. You will work harder at drawing others out. When you do this, you are giving someone permission to come out from behind their mask. You are offering someone a safe zone to open up. This is the secret to having an outward-focused life. This is what it means to *"Be Eucharist"* for someone! This is how, collectively as Christians, we can change the world. We must get the notion out of our hearts that we are the only person with wounds and brokenness and the only one with secrets on a Purple Paper. Everyone has them, and everyone hides them.

Please, if you forget everything else in this book, do not forget this. I never will. If Bob had not cared enough to keep trying, three times, to help me, if he had not persisted, if he had not cared, I possibly would have never gained the courage to tell anyone about my wounds and brokenness, and the chains of sin would likely still be holding me captive. God worked through Bob. Because of Bob, God worked a miracle in my life. I will be forever grateful.

In 1 John 4:7-8, we read, *"Beloved, let us love one another, because love is of God; everyone who loves is begotten by God and knows God. Whoever is without love does not know God, for God is love."* John continues in verse 9 by telling us that the love of God was revealed when He sent His Son into the world. Still further on in verse 11, John gives us a very important principle of Christian life. He says, *"Beloved, if God so loved us, we also **must** love one another."* Pay particular attention to the fact this was not a suggestion; it was a command.

We read this same command to love in John 15:12-16. Let me break it down.

In verse 12, Jesus says, *"This is my commandment: love one another **as I love you**."* Something very important is being revealed here. If we are commanded to love as Jesus loved, then we must look to what He did.

Verse 13 states, *"No one has greater love than this, to lay down one's life for one's friends."*

Verse 14, Jesus tells us plainly, *"You are my friends if you do what I command you."* No doubt we want to be Jesu's friend, so what is He commanding us to do?

We find that key in verse 16," *It was not you who chose me, but I who chose you and appointed you to go and bear fruit that will remain."*

Notice who acted first. God chose us. It was not the other way around. He chose us for what? He chose us to bear fruit. How do we do that? By loving like He did. How do we do that? By seeking out others and loving them. We must be the ones who seek them out. That is what my friend Bob did for me. Laying down our life for others means putting them first. Every day you encounter people who are metaphorically carrying their own Purple Paper around in their pocket.

Are you ready to break someone else's chains? Are you prepared to go out today to take the good news of Jesus to others? Will you care for them, like Jesus cares for you? In time, if you make this a way of life, one day, it will become easier for you to remove your own mask and reveal your own Purple Paper. This requires trust. Please trust me on this, but more importantly, trust God.

BECOMING EUCHARIST

We have been *chosen* by God! We are *blessed*. We are *broken*. God wants us to be *shared*. Everything up to this point in the book has been written to lead us to this one fundamental point. You and I have been called to become Eucharist, Communion, or The Last Supper, whichever term you prefer, to a world starving to receive Christ.

Writing this chapter was quite a challenge. As I said at the beginning, I wrote this book for all Christians. I want this book to cross denominational lines. I wanted it to be ecumenical. With that said, there is no doubt that Catholics hold a unique view of the Eucharistic meal. For me, as a Catholic, the Eucharist is the source and summit of my faith. The Catholic Church holds to the belief that the Eucharist is the real presence of Jesus in the world today. Clearly, God is spiritually present in the world, everywhere and always. All Christians can agree on that. For Catholics, however, the Eucharist is something extraordinarily special. The Eucharist is the real physical presence of Jesus Christ.

John 6:53-58 says, *"Jesus said to them, 'Amen, amen, I say to you, unless you eat the flesh of the Son of Man and drink his blood, you do not have life within you. Whoever eats my flesh and drinks my blood has eternal life, and I will raise him on the last day. For my flesh is true food, and my blood is true drink. Whoever eats my flesh and drinks my blood remains in me and I in him. Just as the living Father sent me and I have life because of the Father, so also the one who feeds on me will have life because of me. This is the bread that came down from heaven. Unlike your ancestors who ate and still died, whoever eats this bread will live forever."*

The divide over the meaning of the Eucharist is nothing new. In John 6:52, we read, *"The Jews quarreled among themselves, saying, 'How can this man give us [his] flesh to eat?'"*

I do not want to downplay the significance of the theological divide, but I also do not want that divide to distract from the meaning I am driving at in this message. My sincerest hope is that we all come to recognize our call to "be Christ" for others in our world today. It has often been said that "Christ has no hands and feet on earth today other than ours."

Granted, the balance of this chapter may resonate more deeply with you if you are a Catholic. But if you are not Catholic or if you are one of the Catholics who struggle to believe in the real presence of Christ in the Eucharist, you should still hear a clarion call of this message to be those hands and feet of Christ to the world.

Throughout the entire section of the book about being shared, I have put forth the premise that it is only when we honestly and, in all humility, admit to others that we are wounded and broken that we "become" Eucharist. Sharing our brokenness transforms us, much like the consecration transforms the bread and wine. Is this idea that we are *"called to be Eucharist"* something new or something that I just made up? Absolutely not! Great theologians have put this idea forth throughout the ages.

Let's go all the way back to the earliest days of Christianity and look at the writings of Irenaeus. He was a Greek from Smyrna in Asia Minor, now a part of Turkey. He was born during the first half of the second century, sometime between 120 and 140. Chosen as bishop of Lugdunum, now Lyon, he is noted for his role in guiding and expanding Christian communities in what is now the south of France and, more widely, for the development of Christian theology by combating heresy and defining orthodoxy. He is recognized as a saint by both the Catholic Church and the Eastern Orthodox Church and remembered by the Church of England. Here is what he said, "When we drink the cup at the Eucharist, in which wine has become Christ's blood, His blood mixes with our blood, and they become one. Equally, when we eat the bread, which has become the body of Christ, His body mixes with our body, and they become one."[15]

Aurelius Augustinus, better known as Augustine of Hippo or Saint Augustine, had this to say on the topic of becoming Eucharist, "I am the food of grown men. Grow, and you shall feed upon me. You will not change me into yourself, as you change food into your flesh, but you will be changed into me!" St. Augustine was born in the year 354. He is recognized as a saint in the Catholic Church, the Eastern Orthodox Church, and the Anglican Communion. He was a theologian, philosopher, and the bishop of Hippo in Roman North Africa. He is considered to be a preeminent Catholic Doctor of the Church and is viewed as one of the most important Church Fathers of the Latin Church. Some consider him to be the most significant Christian thinker after St. Paul.

Now let's turn our attention to Thomas Aquinas. Born in the year 1224, he was a Dominican friar, philosopher, Catholic priest, and Doctor of the Church. He is considered to be one of the Catholic Church's greatest theologians, and he was an enormously influential philosopher. He is recognized as a saint in the Roman Catholic Church and venerated in the Anglican Communion and Lutheran Church.

This is his viewpoint on us being Eucharist, "Material food, first of all, turns itself into the person who eats it, and as a consequence, restores his losses and increases his vital energies. Spiritual food, on the other hand, turns the person who eats it into Itself, and thus the proper effect of this sacrament is the conversion of man into Christ, so that he may no longer live for himself, but that Christ may live in him. And as a consequence, it has the double effect of restoring the spiritual losses caused by sins and defects and of increasing the power of the virtues."

Jumping forward to our modern age, Pope Benedict XVI had this to say in 2007 in his exhortation *Sacramentum Caritatis*, "Each of us is truly called, together with Jesus, to be bread broken for the life of the world."[16]

In his general audience on February 12, 2014, Pope Francis said this, "Through the Eucharist, however, Christ wishes to enter into our life and permeate it with His grace, so that in every Christian community there may be coherence between liturgy and life." He points out that Jesus' life was an act of total sharing of Himself out of love. For Jesus this meant sharing the desires, problems, and issues that agitated the souls of His disciples. Pope Francis went on to say, "Jesus asks us also to forgive and to give. To be instruments of mercy because it was we who first received mercy from God."[17]

Finally, in 2019, Bishop Robert Barron, in his book *Letter to a Suffering Church*, had this to say, "When we consume the Eucharist, we are taking the whole Christ—body, blood, soul, and divinity—into ourselves, becoming thereby conformed to Him in the most literal sense. Through this great sacrament, we are Christified, eternalized, deified, made ready for life on high with God."[18]

So, you can clearly see that this idea of *"becoming Eucharist"* is nothing new. From the earliest days of Christianity until now, we, as Christians, have been called to become what we eat. When we consume the body of Christ, we are expected to go out, and through our very lives, become Eucharist for those starving for the good news of Jesus Christ.

THE BLOOD OF CHRIST

Then James and John, the sons of Zebedee, came to him and said to him, "Teacher, we want you to do for us whatever we ask of you." He replied, "What do you wish [me] to do for you?" They answered him, "Grant that in your glory we may sit one at your right and the other at your left." Jesus said to them, "You do not know what you are asking. Can you drink the cup that I drink or be baptized with the baptism with which I am baptized?" They said to him, "We can." Jesus said to them, "The cup that I drink, you will drink, and with the baptism with which I am baptized, you will be baptized; but to sit at my right or at my left is not mine to give but is for those for whom it has been prepared." - Mark 10:35-40

Hopefully, by now, I have presented a strong case that, like the bread at the last supper, you and I are also blessed, broken, and meant to be shared. Catholic author Henri J.M. Nouwen in his book, *Can You Drink the Cup*, makes the case that we are also challenged to live our lives like the cup of wine shared by Christ at the Last Supper.

Nouwen puts forth that we each only have one life to live. In a similar way, we only have one cup. This cup is emblematic of our life. First, we are called to hold our cup. Like a wine connoisseur studies the look and color of the wine in his cup, we must muster the courage to take a critical look at our life.

There are many varieties of wine, and there is an endless variety of human lives. We are but one. We only have the opportunity to drink our own cup. When we peer into our cup, it is filled with all of the joys and sorrows that make up our life. We don't have the opportunity to drink someone else's cup, and no one can drink ours. Nouwen says that when we look into our cup, we must say, "This is my cup that was given to me."

Next, we must raise our cup. In his book, Nouwen goes on to point out that in the many cultures around the world, there are many different things said when a group of people raise their glasses together in a salute. Here in the United States, we commonly say, "Cheers." However, he points out that it is a Jewish custom to say *"L'chaim."* L'chaim means "To life." In other words, when we clink our glasses together, I am saluting your life, and you are saluting mine. Here he writes, "The wounds of our individual lives, which seemed intolerable when lived alone, become sources of healing when we live them as part of a fellowship of mutual care."[19] In essence, he is confirming the importance of being in a small group and being part of a strong Christian community, as I stated earlier in the book.

Eventually, we must put the cup to our lips and drink it. Here Nouwen suggests that we might protest. We might say, "Why do I have to be this person?"[20] As to our cup, he states, "I didn't ask for it, and I don't want it."

He goes on to say, "As we gradually come to befriend our own reality, to look with compassion at our own sorrows and joys, and as we are able to discover the unique potential of our way of being in the world, we can move beyond our protest, put the cup of our life to our lips and drink it, slowly, carefully but fully. Drink to the dregs!"[21]

Friends, he is so right—we must accept the reality that we are flawed people. It does us no good to hide it. In fact, it hurts us and hurts others when we try to disguise our true selves to others. Once we begin encouraging others to share their wounds, brokenness, and the dire need for Jesus with us, and we, in turn, share our wounds, brokenness, and the need for Jesus with them, we can finally all begin to heal. Together we can grow closer in community with each other and with God. This is what it means to be BLESSED, BROKEN, and SHARED. This is what it means to *"be Eucharist."* This is what it means to become the Body of Christ.

Are you ready?

MUSIC MEDITATION

Before heading into the final two chapters, I urge you to download and drink in the deeply moving words of the song *"How Beautiful"* by Twila Paris.

Not only did the beautiful hands of Jesus offer up the bread at the Last Supper, but His hands, feet, and side were also pierced for our sins. He is our Beautiful Savior! Now God is calling you and me to go out and become the beautiful hands and feet of Christ to those we meet.

Will we answer His call?

HAUNTED BY THE STORY OF THE LITTLE BOY

After this, Jesus went across the Sea of Galilee [of Tiberias]. A large crowd followed him, because they saw the signs he was performing on the sick. Jesus went up on the mountain, and there he sat down with his disciples. The Jewish feast of Passover was near. When Jesus raised his eyes and saw that a large crowd was coming to him, he said to Philip, "Where can we buy enough food for them to eat?" He said this to test him, because he himself knew what he was going to do.

Philip answered him, "Two hundred days' wages worth of food would not be enough for each of them to have a little [bit]." One of his disciples, Andrew, the brother of Simon Peter, said to him, [9]"There is a boy here who has five barley loaves and two fish; but what good are these for so many?" Jesus said, "Have the people recline." Now there was a great deal of grass in that place. So the men reclined, about five thousand in number. Then Jesus took the loaves, gave thanks, and distributed them to those who were reclining, and also as much of the fish as they wanted. When they had had their fill, he said to his disciples, "Gather the fragments left over, so that nothing will be wasted." So they collected them, and filled twelve wicker baskets with fragments from the five barley loaves that had been more than they could eat. When the people saw the sign he had done, they said, "This is truly the Prophet, the one who is to come into the world." Since Jesus knew that they were going to come and carry him off to make him king, he withdrew again to the mountain alone. - John 6:1-15

This sixth chapter of John's Gospel is so rich in its message to us and is packed with symbolism. I hope to be able to tie the main points of this entire book together by examining one key aspect of this story, namely, the actions of the little boy we read about in verse 9. Let's take a look at some of those symbols and what they might mean for us as we strive to be the door through which others encounter Christ. And then, let's focus on the little boy.

To begin with, it says in verse 3 that the people were on a mountain. This point cannot be glossed over. Remember that the Garden of Eden was on a mountain, and the rivers flowed forth from the garden. Abraham took Isaac to Mount Moriah to be sacrificed. Moses received the commandments on Mount Sinai. According to tradition, the transfiguration took place on Mount Tabor. God's Holy City of Jerusalem is on Mount Zion, and finally, Jesus was crucified on Mount Calvary.

Throughout the Bible, great things took place on mountains. People would go up to the mountains, and God would come down to the mountains. Mountains were places where God and man came together for their encounters. John knew this, and therefore he included this detail in this story to emphasize the importance of what took place.

In verse 3, John tells us that Jesus sat down. Sitting was the traditional position rabbis assumed to teach the people. It has long been said that actions speak louder than words. Jesus was about to teach with both words and actions as He performed this amazing miracle before a very large crowd.

We are told, in verse 4, *"The Jewish feast of Passover was near."* Each year the Jewish people would celebrate Passover in remembrance of their liberation from slavery in Egypt. Jesus was preparing the people for the New Passover that would soon take place in which He would be the sacrificial lamb.

Bishop Robert Barron once said in a homily that John was painting a picture of the mass in this first part of John 6. First, Jesus preaches to the people. Catholics would be quick to recognize this as the Liturgy of the Word. Next, Jesus feeds the people. Catholics might see this as the foretelling of the Liturgy of the Eucharist.

John also added what seems to be a minor point that could easily be overlooked. In verse 9, he tells us that the bread was made from barley. I have read that, in those days, unlike bread made from wheat, bread made from barley was more commonly associated with the poor. Because bread made from barley was seen as the food of the poor, John might also be using this seemingly minor point to tell us that the little boy who came forward was from a poor family and gave all they had. John also ties this story to 2 Kings 4:42, which says, *"A man came from Baal-shalishah bringing the man of God twenty barley loaves made from the first fruits, and fresh grain in the ear."*

Notice in verse 11 Jesus took the loaves and gave thanks. This correlates to what Jesus would do with the bread at the Last Supper.

The story concludes in verse 13 when John tells us that there were twelve baskets left over. Twelve was the figure of fullness or abundance. John might be giving us a metaphor for the abundance of God manifested in His abundant grace, His abundant mercy, and His abundant forgiveness. Twelve also ties into the twelve tribes of Israel.

Clearly, the story of the multiplication of the loaves and fishes is one of the most widely known stories in the New Testament. It is so important that it appears in all four Gospels. Many of these symbols are depicted in the other Gospels. There is, however, something different about John's version of the story. It is only in the Gospel of John that we discover where the loaves and fishes came from. In verse 9, we read, ***"There is a boy here who has five barley loaves and two fish."***

Please, for a few moments, permit me the literary license to embellish a few of the details of this very familiar story for the purpose of making my point.

Okay, here we go…. Let's assume for a minute that you are the father of the little boy. You have been hearing about this rabbi named Jesus for some time now. You have heard about the miracles of healing that He has performed. You have also heard that this rabbi can tell stories for a long time. Knowing this, you and your family planned well for this outing.

You packed some blankets to sit on and a basket of food, enough for your entire family and a few of your relatives who were planning to go out to listen to Jesus with you. You packed five barley loaves and two fish.

As a result of planning ahead and arriving early, your family had front-row seats on the grassy mountainside that day. You were right up near the rabbi and His disciples. Now, settled, you listened with great interest to this charismatic speaker named Jesus. He seemed to speak to your soul. You were, however, continually distracted and annoyed by others in the crowd who murmured criticism of Jesus. As you glanced over at a few loud skeptics in the crowd, you missed an important interaction between Jesus and His Disciples. Although you were temporarily distracted by the grumblings of the crowd, your very attentive son overheard the conversation. This is what he heard, "Where can we buy enough food for them to eat?" He also heard the reply, "Two hundred days' wages worth of food would not be enough for each of them to have a little bit."

Without a moment's hesitation, your son grabbed the family's food basket and ran up to one of the disciples named Andrew and said, *"Sir, here is our food. Will this help you feed this crowd?"*

Now, if you were like most dads, you might have yelled out, *"Son, get back here. That is our food. Let those other people fend for themselves."* But it was too late. Jesus was already taking the basket that Andrew was handing Him.

So, what is the point of my additional embellishments to the story? To answer that question, allow me to ask you a question. Did Jesus need anything from anybody in order to feed the crowd? In other words, did Jesus need kindling wood to start a fire? No, of course not. Jesus is God; He could have snapped His fingers, and the entire crowd could have received a delicious steak dinner, complete with all of the trimmings accompanied with forks, knives, and napkins, and even a delicious dessert. But that has traditionally not been how God works.

God most often works through people who respond to His call. We see this depicted in the many great figures who appear throughout the entire Old Testament. In other words, God performs miracles when people act. He is prepared to work those miracles through us, too, if we respond to His call.

It has been over two thousand years since Jesus performed the miracle of the multiplication of the loaves and fishes. Ponder this question. Would we even know about that day on the mountain and the multiplication of the loaves and fishes if that young boy had not offered up their family food basket? Would the crowd have gone home hungry that day? Have you ever wondered why

John, unlike the other Gospel writers, gave us this important detail about the little boy?

Now, think about this as well. How did the boy's action impact the boy himself? He and his family would have eaten their fill that day. If you think about it, neither the boy nor his family was directly impacted by the miracle that day. They would have had their food even without the miracle. This makes this story all the more poignant to the main point in this book.

Throughout human history, God has done marvelous things—yes, including miracles—when people have responded to His call. Sometimes when people respond to God's call, He works through those people to perform miracles in someone else's life. God worked through the unselfish act of the little boy to work a miracle in the lives of thousands of people on that mountain that day, and that is why we still know about those events over two thousand years later.

God delights in our participation. Jesus did not need the boy's bread. The boy presented all he had to offer. Jesus took what the boy offered and multiplied it. You could even say He transubstantiated it and fed the crowd with the bread of life.

Now, stop and think back about my friend Bob. Bob responded to the promptings of the Holy Spirit when he reached out to me three times. As a result, I received a healing miracle that day. Bob's life would have been no different if he had not acted, but I would have lost out on a miracle.

Many years ago, Fr. Nick, who I mentioned earlier in the book, gave a homily on this story. He said something in his homily that has stuck with me throughout the years. He said, "I want you HAUNTED by the story of the little boy." I was startled by that remark. I have never heard anyone say that about anything in the Bible before or since. Here is why he said it.

Imagine for a moment that this very day, God is planning to work a miracle in someone's life, but that miracle will only happen if you respond to God's promptings. If you fail to respond and just go about your business, as usual, you probably will not notice any difference in your life. Your life will not be negatively impacted because of your inaction. However, someone else will lose out on the miracle God was hoping to provide them. This thought should haunt all of us!

We must ask ourselves, "Are we willing to be like the little boy?" Are we willing to recognize a need in someone's life and allow God the opportunity to work through us to heal them? This is how we live a life that is Blessed, Broken, and Shared. But if we just keep to ourselves, we should be haunted by the reality that an isolated Christian is an ineffective evangelizer.

One boy's action allowed God to feed thousands. What could God do through us if we respond to His promptings and genuinely ask how someone is truly doing? What if we even go so far as to share our lives simply, honestly, vulnerably, and completely by sharing our joys, struggles, fears, and failures with them? Will we, by doing so, give others the courage to share their brokenness with us and, as a result, allow the healing power of Christ to reach them in their pain? God is ready to perform more miracles today. He is just waiting for you and me to act.

Let me ask you this as the book is drawing nearer to the end. I have written a great deal about our wounds and brokenness. I have emphasized bringing those things we hide in the dark to the light of day. I have talked about the importance of helping others do the same. I know that the thought of doing so is scary because

I was scared. So, what thoughts have you scared, all stirred up right now? What strong winds are blowing in your life and causing you fear? Listen carefully to what Jesus is speaking to your soul. He is saying to you the same thing that He said 365 times throughout the Bible, *"Do not be afraid."*

So, where does this leave us? We are left with the truth that Jesus is the Son of God. He is the source of everlasting life. He is the true bread that comes down from Heaven. We are told that when we believe in Him that He will be in us. We have been told that He alone is the source of eternal life.

We also know we are blessed by His mercy, love, and forgiveness. We know we have been commissioned to go forth to tell others. We know that people are starving to be fed. We know that if they feast on Jesus that they will never grow hungry or thirsty again.

We know that even though we are a broken door, people can enter through us to encounter Jesus, the perfect door to the Father. But we must act in order to be that door. We must live open, honest, and transparent lives, and we must help others do so as well.

I am asking you to become Eucharist for others. I am asking you to live your life blessed, broken, and shared. Will you do this, or will you, as many on that day did, murmur and return to your old ways of life? God has called us, but He has also given us free will and given us the ability to reject His call. What will you do?

If Jesus were to ask you, like He did the twelve apostles, *"Do you also want to leave?"* How will you answer Him? My hope is that you will say, *"Master, to whom shall we go? You have the words of eternal life. We have come to believe and are convinced that you are the Holy One of God."*

So, I ask you now, will you help people find Jesus? He is the one that has the words of everlasting life. If you and I live a shared, open, and transparent life that truly reflects our need for and love of, Jesus and if we make others feel safe to open up about their trials, wounds, and brokenness, then they can truly have an encounter with the Lord. By admitting our brokenness and dependence on Jesus, we give others the courage to do the same. When we do, a miracle might take place in their life because of you.

GOING FORTH

Please allow me to recap a few of the key points of the book.
- We are called to be a door, no matter how broken we might be, through which others can enter to encounter Christ.
- Mercy and forgiveness are God's greatest blessings to us.
- All people are either broken by their own sin, wounded by living in a broken and sinful world, or both.
- We are all chained by some recurring sin in our life.
- Most, if not all, people are scared to reveal their brokenness to others.
- Jesus came to save the lost and broken.
- We all have a Purple Paper with well-kept secrets written on it.
- We are all living in a virtual Sea of Purple.
- We all wear a mask to hide the real us from others.
- Satan often uses the "yellow paper mask" to keep us overly focused on the wrong sins.
- Most of us are living life Blessed, Broken, and Scared.
- As Christians, we are called to be Eucharist for others starving for Jesus Christ.

- If we want to be healed, we have to tell someone we are broken.
- In order to be Eucharist for others, we all need to live our lives Blessed, Broken, and SHARED.
- Each of us is truly called, together with Jesus, to be bread broken for the life of the world.
- The more conscious we are of our own wounds and brokenness, the more capable we will be at looking upon others with acceptance and mercy.
- Like Christ, we are called to be wounded healers.
- We cannot be effective in ministry unless we know and u derstand that everyone is broken, and we are, too.
- God intends for us to live life in Christian community. Being a member of a small group that meets weekly is an ideal way to build solid Christian friendships in a safe place where we can share our joys, struggles, pains, and broke ness.
- God works miracles through us when we act on His promptings—as we see in the little boy who offers up the loaves and fish in John 6:9. Be the boy!

Dear friends, we are living in a virtual "Sea of Purple." All around us, each day, we encounter people who are wearing masks to hide the pain of their wounds and brokenness. God is calling us to be sharing and caring people. With the recognition that all people are broken, we should worry that if we neglect our responsibility to reach out to them, if we fail to provide an open environment for safe sharing, these people will continue to hurt alone. They'll miss the miracle God has in store for them. If we do not act, you and I will be the cause of the miracle that never happened. That possibility should leave us all haunted by the story of the little boy.

WILL YOU BE THE LITTLE BOY FOR SOMEONE?

STANDING IN THE STORMS OF LIFE

Permit me to share one last quote from Christian author Adam S. McHugh that wraps up the essence of this entire book, using the image of a storm to make the point. Here is what he says, "A hurting person is in a storm. They are cold, wet, shivering, and scared. Preaching, platitudes, and advice will not get them out of the storm. Don't tell a person in a storm that it's a sunny day. There will likely come a day when the clouds part, but it is not today. It's not your job to pull them out of the storm. It's your job to get wet with them."[22]

Let's begin today. Let's make a new resolution to live our lives in communion with others. Let's take our masks off. Let's respond like the little boy. Let's be the broken door through which others can enter to encounter Christ. Let's be willing to get wet with others who are stuck in the storms of life. **And finally, let us go forth as Blessed, Broken, and Shared people so that we can become Eucharist for a world starving for Jesus. He is the Bread of Life, the one who offers those who believe in Him eternal life.**

I'M BROKEN, YOU'RE BROKEN, GOD'S NOT, LET'S TALK!

ENDNOTES

[1] Augustine of Hippo, *Confessions*, 2002, New City Press

[2] The London Daily News, August 16, 1905

[3] Clive Staples Lewis, *The Great Divorce A Dream*, 1954, HarperCollins, p99

[4] Pope Francis, *The Name Of God Is Mercy*, 2016, Random House Publishing Group, p34

[5] Pope Francis, *The Name Of God Is Mercy*, 2016, Random House Publishing Group, p33

[6] Pope Francis, *The Name Of God Is Mercy*, 2016, Random House Publishing Group

[7] Scott Hahn, *The Lamb's Supper*, 1999, Doubleday, p110

[8] America Magazine Sept. 19, 2013, *"A Big Heart Open to God,"*

[9] Pope Francis, *The Name Of God Is Mercy*, 2016, Random House Publishing Group

[10] Dietrich Bonhoeffer, *Life Together: The Classic Exploration of Faith in Community*, 1978, HarperOne

[11] St. Catherine of Siena, *The Dialogue*, Paulist Press, 1980

[12] R. W. Emerson: *English Traits Representative Men and Other Essays*, 1932, J.M. Dent & Sons

[13] Pope Francis, *The Name Of God Is Mercy*, 2016, Random House Publishing Group. p67

[14] Pope Francis, *General Audience in St. Peter's Square*, November 21, 2018

[15] Frank T. Griswold, *Praying Our Days,* 2009, Morehouse Publishing, p73

[16] Pope Benedict XVI, *Sacramentum Caritatis,* 2007

[17] Pope Francis, *General Audience Address,* February 12, 2014

[18] Bishop Robert Barron, *Letter to a Suffering Church,* 2019,

[19] Henri J.M. Nouwen, *Can You Drink the Cup,* 2006. Ave Maria Press, p87

[20] Henri J.M. Nouwen, *Can You Drink the Cup,* 2006. Ave Maria Press, p87

[21] Henri J.M. Nouwen, *Can You Drink the Cup,* 2006. Ave Maria Press, p87

[22] Adam S. McHugh, *The Listening Life: Embracing Attentiveness in a World of Distraction,* 2015 (IVP Books), p161

NOTES

EXERCISE ONE & TWO CARDS

Purple Paper

Yellow Paper